EAT CHEAPLY

FABULOUS FOODS for

Pennies a Portion

by Dorothy R. Bates

This book is dedicated to everyone who loves good food. Special thanks to my daughter, Kathy Hill, who edited the book, and to my son, Albert Bates, who formatted it for me.

Published in the United States by The Magni Group, Inc.
P.O.Box 849 McKinney TX 75070
Printed in the United States of America

ISBN: 1-882330-06-4

Contents

Introduction

"What would you cook if Julia Child were coming to your house for dinner?"

That's the question an enterprising reporter for the San Antonio Express asked several professional cooks at the annual convention of The International Association of Culinary Professionals. (For one of the replies, see the recipe for Individual Meat Loaves with Topping Sauce.)

What would you cook? What would I cook? One of life's greatest pleasures is sharing a good home-cooked meal wih friends. Cooking the meal need not be expensive or difficult. Here are dozens of delightful dinners planned for you and your friends, and shopping for any one of them can be done for less than ten dollars— I've done it.

We share a rich and diverse cultural heritage with a repertoire of recipes ranging from ethnic to regional to international, from cherished family recipes to recent ones exchanged with friends. We cook in a global kitchen with a world of ingredients and seasonings at our fingertips. We try out trendy new dishes, but often long for good old-fashioned comfort foods. We are health conscious, but we occasionally yearn for a rich, downright fattening dessert.

Planning the Meal

Combining something traditional with something new adds zest and a conversation piece to a dinner. Some meals may take one to two hours to prepare; some can be done in very little time. Choose a menu you would enjoy eating and have the satisfaction of cooking it.

Some of my best recipes came from the spattered pages of much-used cookbooks, but have been revised to use less fat or fewer eggs. Many recipes were given to me by friends; some were inspired by magazine articles.

Most of these recipes serve four, but can be doubled if you wish to serve dinner for eight. Many of the desserts, such as cakes and pies, serve more than four, and are perfect to take to a potluck supper.

The fragrant aroma of freshly baked bread or rolls says "welcome" and adds that extra touch of caring to a marvelous meal. Yeast breads are easy to make; you just have to allow time for the dough to rise. Quick breads, like muffins or drop biscuits, take very little time, but will add a touch of warmth to your menu.

You can be flexible in menu planning; trying different hot breads or different desserts with this or that main dish. You may find one little hot roll or bread, or a certain dessert, that becomes your signature dish.

Keeping It Simple

To keep entertaining dinner guests simple and stress free, so the cook enjoys the meal as much as others do:

• Choose a menu several days in advance
• Prepare a grocery list of ingredients needed
• Shop two days ahead
• Make one or more recipes the day before
• Set the table the night before

Set a pretty table, using your best china and glassware. Polish up grandmother's silver or brass candlesticks. Arrange a centerpiece of fresh or dried flowers, fruit or a potted plant.

You can create a bistro atmosphere with a red-checked tablecloth, set a mood of old-world elegance with a lace or damask cloth, or strike a contemporary note with colorful place mats. Cloth napkins provide an accent color, and along with your centerpiece, help to dress up the table. Keep the preparations simple, so both hosts and guests will enjoy the wonderful home-cooked food.

Keeping Food Costs Down

Check newspaper ads for supermarket specials. Freeze chicken or chops when these are on sale. If "Family pack" is the best buy, divide the contents into smaller packages to freeze. Clip coupons, and use them where you get double or triple value. Buy fruits and vegetables in season when possible; these cost least and taste best.

Buy spices and grains at a whole foods store where they are available in bulk. For example: a 1-ounce jar of dill weed cost $4.49 at a local supermarket, but dill weed at a natural foods store was 81 cents an ounce. One ounce will last several months. Herbs and spices add a lot of zing to simple dishes and are inexpensive when bought in bulk.

Almonds, walnuts and pecans can be bought in bulk, too, and will keep fresh for months in the freezer. Take out the amount needed for a recipe. Flavors are enhanced if the nuts are toasted just before using. Spread chopped nuts on a dish and toast for a minute or two in a microwave oven, watching so they do not burn, or spread out on a pie plate and toast in a moderate oven for 10 minutes.

The Happy Ending: Dessert

Whether you choose to serve an elegant and elaborate looking (but easy to make) dessert, like Walnut Meringue Cake with Pineapple Filling, or something simple and light like Lemon Cheese Pie, a homemade dessert makes the meal memorable. It's an excuse to linger at the candlelit table for conversation, perhaps sipping after-dinner coffee or tea. Here's a hint: put some orange peel and a stick of cinnamon in the pot with the ground coffee for a subtle taste of expensive gourmet coffee.

So, invite friends over, choose a menu, shop with care, cook part of the meal ahead—an evening of pleasure awaits.

What would I cook for Julia Child? Maybe Chicken Tetrazzini, or Deviled Pork Chops, or perhaps the Golden Mediterranean Stew....it would be hard to choose from this rich and varied collection of my favorite recipes.

MENUS

Beef Stroganoff on Noodles
Zucchini Italian Style
Lettuce and Tomato Salad
Crusty French Bread
Walnut Meringue Cake with Pineapple Filling

Chinese Chicken and Walnuts
Basmati Rice
Sesame Cucumber Salad
Lemon-Glazed Monkey Bread
Peach Cobbler Supreme

Deviled Pork Chops
Crisp Roast Potatoes
Maple Glazed Carrots
Coleslaw with Yogurt Dressing
Seeded Rye Rolls
Lemon Squares

Chicken Tetrazzini
Baby Peas with Mint
Garlic Toasts
Green Salad with Herb Dressing
French Apple Cake

Cheese Strata Romanoff
Lemon Broccoli
Baked Tomato Halves
Whole Wheat Honey Rolls
Strawberry Meringue Tarts

Jambalaya with Ham and Rice
Cucumber and Lettuce Salad
Raspberry Jam Muffins
Apple Oatmeal Crisp

Golden Mediterranean Vegetable Stew
Fluffy Couscous
Spring Salad with French Dressing
Orange Bowknot Rolls
Chocolate Mint Squares

Shrimp Fettuccine
Spinach Orange Salad and Ginger Dressing
Herbed Pita Bread Triangles
Date Walnut Cake

Chicken Almond Rice Casserole
Grapefruit and Avocado Salad
Lemon Honey Dressing
Dilly Cheese Rolls
Blueberry Buckle

Tamale Pie
Cauliflower with Crumb Topping
Two-Green Salad with Apple
Chocolate Pudding Cake

Spinach-Stuffed Shells
Williamsburg Cabbage Salad
Breadsticks with Sesame Seeds
Magic Coconut Pie

Individual Meat Loaves
Parsley Potatoes
Green Beans with Mushrooms
Buttermilk Biscuits
Chocolate Pecan Pie

Broccoli Bisque
Focaccia with Onions and Walnuts
Greek Salad
Poppy Seed Loaf Cake

Szechwan Shrimp
Lettuce Salad with Green Dressing
Herbed French Bread
Lemon Pudding Cakes

Provençal Beans with Dill
Red and Yellow Tomato Salad
Jalapeño Corn Muffins
Pineapple Ice Box Dessert

Chicken Paprika on Noodles
Green Beans Lyonnaise
Romaine Salad with Herb Croutons
Strawberry Shortcakes

Oven-Crisp Fish Nuggets
Baked Stuffed Potatoes
Broccoli Italian Style
Garden Salad with Chutney Dressing
Nesselrode Pie with Chocolate Curls

Stuffed Green Peppers
Country Corn Pudding
Molded Cucumber Salad
Onion Rolls
Poached Pears with Chocolate Sauce

Cantonese Beef and Vegetables
Blueberry Muffins
Apple Upside-down Tart
Vanilla Sauce

Chicken Pie with Cornbread Topping
Sweet Potatoes with Pecans
Grapefruit Red Pepper Salad
Orange Soy Dressing
Banana Nut Cake with Cream Cheese Icing

Baked Cheese Enchiladas
Mexican Rice
Refried Beans
Pink Onion Rings
Strawberry Cream Pie

Linguine with Fresh Asparagus
Tomato Aspic Salad
Zucchini Muffins
Fresh Peach Melba

Fish Fillets Vera Cruz
Rice and Onion Pilaf
Romaine Salad with Avocado Dressing
Skillet Corn Bread
Lemon Yogurt Cake

Beef Ragout
Mashed Potatoes with Carrots
Summer Squash Medley
Lettuce with Thousand Island Dressing
White Chocolate Pie

Chicken Curry on Rice
Assorted Condiments
Cucumber Raita
Apple or Peach Chutney
Angel Biscuits
Forgotten Cookies with Sherbet

London Pub Cabbage Pie
Braised Carrots and Onions
Waldorf Salad with Almonds
Irish Soda Bread
Strawberry Rhubarb Crumble

Super Spicy Baked Chicken
Zucchini Rice Pilaf
Asian Cabbage Salad
Refrigerator Rolls
Pineapple Apricot Upside-down Cake

Sweet and Pungent Pork
Chow Mein Noodles
Marinated Tomato Salad
Scallion Drop Biscuits
Lemon Cheese Pie

Chiles Relleno American Style
Baked Stuffed Tomatoes
Brazilian Black Bean Salad
Brown Rice Breadsticks
Cherry Cake with Streusel Topping

Individual Salmon Loaves with Dill Sauce
Oven Crisp Potato Cubes
Green Beans with Almonds
Carrot Raisin Salad
Peach Cream Pie

Jamaican Lentils with Rice
Beets in Orange Sauce
Cucumber Dill Salad
Baked Bananas
Oatmeal Chocolate Chip Cookies

Meatballs Carbonade on Noodles
Pattypan Squash Sauté
Freezable Cabbage Slaw
Rhubarb Cream Pie

Chicken Breasts in Supreme Sauce
Golden Potato Slices
Green Beans Vinaigrette
Fudge Brownie Pie

Beef Stroganoff on Noodles
Zucchini Italian Style
Lettuce and Tomato Salad
Crusty French Bread
Walnut Meringue Cake with Pineapple Filling

Beef Stroganoff

Serves 4

This dish is a great continental favorite. It is easy to slice the meat into thin strips if the beef is frozen.

3/4 pound beef sirloin
1/4 cup flour
1/2 teaspoon salt
1/4 teaspoon pepper
2 tablespoons butter or margarine
4 ounces mushrooms, sliced
1 cup beef broth or consommé
2 tablespoons catsup
1 teaspoon Worcestershire sauce
3/4 cup sour cream, at room temperature
12 ounces broad noodles
Fresh parsley for garnish

- Slice beef into thin strips 2 inches long and 1/2 inch wide.
- Roll strips in the flour mixed with salt and pepper.
- Heat half the butter in a hot skillet and lightly fry the mushrooms. Remove.
- Heat pan, add remaining butter, quickly brown the beef.
- Pour in the broth, catsup and Worcestershire, cover pan; simmer until meat is tender, about 30 minutes.
- Add mushrooms to the pan, and when the mixture boils up, remove from heat. Stir in the sour cream and have a warmed platter ready.
- Cook noodles in 4 quarts of boiling salted water. Drain. Arrange noodles on a platter and pour stroganoff over, or divide among individual plates.
- Garnish platter or plates with sprigs of parsley.

Zucchini Italian Style

Serves 4

An Italian friend made this for me years ago, and I've made it often since. Oval slices are attractive, flavors great.

3 small zucchini (about 12 ounces)
1 medium onion, chopped
3 cloves garlic, thinly sliced
2 tablespoons olive oil
1/2 teaspoon salt

- Wash zucchini and trim ends. Slice thinly on the diagonal so you have long oval slices.
- Have onion and garlic ready.
- Heat a large skillet or wok, add oil and swirl around to coat bottom of pan. Have pan fairly hot.
- Sprinkle onions in pan, add zucchini; keep it in a single layer as much as possible.
- Cook 2 minutes, turn slices, sprinkle on the garlic and salt.
- Cook 1 to 2 minutes more. Stir very gently. Don't overcook; squash should be tender but still firm.

Lettuce and Tomato Salad

Serves 4

A crisp salad refreshes the palate and may contain any assortment of the many lettuces available today. The flavor of a vine-ripened tomato provides a tangy accent. Have everything ready to toss with the dressing just before serving.

4 to 5 cups romaine, butter, Bibb or leaf lettuces
1 large tomato or 2 small ones
2 tablespoons vinegar
1/4 teaspoon salt
1/4 teaspoon prepared mustard
4 tablespoons olive oil
Pinch of black pepper

- Wash lettuce and dry with a towel. Tear into bite-size pieces.
- Keep covered and chilled until serving time.
- Wash tomato and remove stem.
- Slice tomato thinly from stem end to bottom. Cut slices in half.
- Mix vinegar with salt and mustard; stir in olive oil and pepper.
- Before serving, stir dressing; toss with tomatoes and lettuce.

Crusty French Bread

Makes 2 loaves

Make the dough one day, bake it the next, and you'll have 2 nice loaves, one to freeze or to make into garlic or herb bread for another meal.

2 teaspoons quick-acting yeast
1 teaspoon sugar
1 cup warm (not hot) water
3 1/2 cups unbleached white flour
1 teaspoon salt
Cornmeal for the baking sheet
nonstick cooking spray

- Add yeast and sugar to the warm water; let stand until foamy.
- Stir in flour and turn dough out on lightly floured surface.
- Knead for 5 minutes, working in more flour as needed, until dough is smooth and elastic.
- Put dough in a lightly oiled bowl, turning around to coat. Cover with a towel and let rise until double, about 1 hour.
- Punch dough down, cover with plastic wrap and refrigerate for at least 8 hours or overnight.
- Remove 4 hours before baking. Spray a baking sheet with nonstick cooking spray and sprinkle with cornmeal.
- Divide dough in half; turn out on a lightly floured surface. Roll out dough into two 12-inch rectangles, roll each up lengthwise, sealing ends and seams tightly. Place dough seam side down on baking sheet. Cover with a towel and let rise until doubled, 1 1/2 to 2 hours.
- Heat oven to 425°.
- Place a pan of hot water in bottom of oven.
- Using scissors or a serrated knife, slash the tops of the loaves about 2 inches apart. Bake 25 to 30 minutes.
- Transfer loaves to a rack to cool.

Walnut Meringue Cake with Pineapple Filling

Serves 10 to 12

This is a showcase dessert of marvelous flavor, easy to make a day ahead. Guests will ask for seconds.

4 eggs, separated
1 2/3 cup sugar, divided
5 tablespoons boiling water
1 cup unbleached white flour
11/2 teaspoons baking powder
1/2 teaspoon lemon extract
1/4 teaspoon cream of tartar
1/2 teaspoon vanilla extract
3/4 cup chopped walnuts

- Line the bottoms of 2 round 8-inch cake pans with circles of waxed paper or parchment paper. Butter the paper.
- Beat egg yolks; gradually add 2/3 cup sugar while beating.
- Add boiling water; beat. Beat in flour and baking powder.
- Add lemon extract. Divide batter evenly into prepared pans.
- Make topping layer by beating the egg whites stiff, and slowly beating in 1 cup sugar, cream of tartar and the vanilla.
- Spread onto batter. Sprinkle walnuts on top of meringue.
- Heat oven to 350° and bake 35 to 40 minutes. Cool on rack.
- Tip out one layer, meringue side down, onto a serving plate.
- Tip out other layer, meringue side down, onto waxed paper. Remove baking papers. Let layers cool.

Filling between layers:

1 can (20 oz.) crushed pineapple, drained
3/4 cup heavy cream for whipping
(or substitute 8 ounces whipped topping)

- Drain pineapple well. Whip cream until stiff.
- Fold pineapple into whipped cream or topping. Spread on bottom layer of cake.
- Carefully place the remaining layer on top of filling, meringue side up. Chill cake 8 hours or overnight.
- Cut cake in wedges to serve.

Chinese Chicken and Walnuts
Basmati Rice
Sesame Cucumber Salad
Lemon-Glazed Monkey Bread
Peach Cobbler Supreme

Chinese Chicken and Walnuts

Stir-frying must be done at the last minute, but you can have all of the ingredients ready ahead of time and invite guests to the kitchen to watch the meal take its final shape.

1 pound chicken breasts or thighs
3 tablespoons soy sauce
1 tablespoon cornstarch
1/2 teaspoon sugar
1/2 cup walnuts, chopped roughly
1 large onion, sliced thinly
1 rib celery, sliced thinly on the diagonal
4 ounces fresh mushrooms, sliced
1 can (8 oz.) water chestnuts, sliced
3 tablespoons oil, divided
1/2 cup chicken broth

- Remove bones and skin from chicken and cut meat in cubes.
- Mix soy sauce, cornstarch and sugar and smear on chicken.
- Heat a large skillet or wok and add 1 tablespoon of oil.
- When oil is hot, add onion slices and celery, cook 3 minutes; add mushrooms, cook 2 minutes; transfer to a bowl.
- Heat pan, add 1 tablespoon oil, and fry walnuts for 3 minutes, stirring so they do not burn. Put walnuts with vegetables.
- Heat pan again, add rest of oil and quickly fry the chicken. Add broth, cover pan, lower heat and cook 10 minutes.
- Add water chestnuts and return the walnuts and vegetables to pan. Stir to mix well and serve hot with rice.

Basmati Rice

Serves 4

Savor the flavor of aromatic basmati rice, originally grown only in the Himalayas. It is available in bulk at whole food stores. Brown rice takes longer to cook, but has a delicious nutty flavor and higher nutritional values.

2 quarts boiling water
1 cup white long grain basmati rice
1/2 teaspoon salt

- Place rice in a strainer and rinse under cold water; drain.
- Bring water to a boil; stir in rice and salt.
- Cook uncovered at a steady boil until the rice is tender, stirring occasionally, 12 to 14 minutes. Taste a grain of rice to check doneness. Strain.

Sesame Cucumber Salad

Serves 4

Ginger root adds zing to this dish, which I learned to make in Chinese cooking classes. In winter, small white turnips can be used instead of cucumbers. Toasting brings out the nutty flavor of sesame seeds.

2 teaspoons sesame seeds
2 medium-size cucumbers
1 teaspoon salt
1/2 cup white vinegar
5 tablespoons sugar
1 tablespoon fresh ginger root, minced

- Place sesame seeds in a small dry skillet and cook about 2 minutes until lightly toasted and fragrant. Set aside.
- Pare the cucumbers, leaving on portions of green. Slice thinly.
- Add salt to cucumbers and let stand 10 minutes.
- Squeeze out the liquid and place cucumbers in a clean bowl.
- Mix in a small saucepan the vinegar, sugar and ginger root. Bring to a boil, stir well and pour over cucumbers.
- Add sesame seeds. Stir and cool.

Lemon-Glazed Monkey Bread

Serves 8

This fragrant hot bread is also called "pull aparts". It's baked in a tube pan, so there are little rolls to tear off the circular "loaf".

1 tablespoon quick-acting yeast
1 cup warm water, divided
2 tablespoons white sugar
1 cup mashed potatoes
1 teaspoon salt
2 tablespoons vegetable oil
2 cups whole wheat flour
1 to 2 cups unbleached white flour
2 tablespoons melted butter or margarine
2 teaspoons lemon juice
3 tablespoons brown sugar
Minced peel of 1 lemon

- Dissolve yeast in warm water with the white sugar and let stand 5 minutes, until foamy. Add mashed potatoes, salt and oil to yeast.
- Stir in flour gradually. Mix well, adding just enough flour so dough is not sticky, but stays soft. Turn out on lightly floured surface and knead for a few minutes, adding flour if needed.
- Place dough in an oiled bowl and turn to coat.
- Cover dough and let rise 1 hour until double.
- Spray a tube pan or bundt pan with nonstick cooking spray.
- Mix brown sugar and finely minced lemon peel.
- Soften butter or margarine, mix in lemon juice.
- Dip small rolls of dough in butter mixture, then in brown sugar. Place rolls in pan, making only 2 layers, (about 24 balls).
- Cover pan and let rise again 40 minutes.
- Heat oven to 350°, bake 30 to 35 minutes; bread will spring back when lightly touched, if done.
- Remove from oven and let cool in pan for 5 minutes.
- Invert pan onto a serving plate. Lift pan off the bread.
- Serve warm. For serving, rolls are torn off with fingers.

Peach Cobbler Supreme

Serves 6

Sometimes a very simple dish is the best dish. This is a favorite at our house when peaches are in season.

6 or 7 fresh peaches
2 tablespoons butter or margarine
1 cup sugar, divided
2 eggs
2 tablespoons water
1 teaspoon vanilla extract
1/2 cup unbleached white flour
1/2 teaspoon baking powder
Dash of nutmeg

- Lightly butter 8 x 8-inch baking dish. Heat oven to 350°.
- Peel peaches and slice into the dish.
- Dot peaches with bits of butter or margarine and half the sugar.
- Use less sugar if peaches are very sweet.
- In a mixing bowl, beat the eggs with the water and vanilla.
- Beat in remaining half cup of sugar, flour and baking powder.
- Spoon batter evenly over peaches. Sprinkle with nutmeg.
- Bake for 30 minutes until top is lightly golden.
- Serve warm or at room temperature.

Deviled Pork Chops
Crisp Roast Potatoes
Maple Glazed Carrots
Coleslaw with Yogurt Dressing
Seeded Rye Rolls
Lemon Squares

Deviled Pork Chops

Serves 4

Marinating lean pork chops in a spicy coating adds flavor and also tenderizes the meat.

4 pork chops, trimmed of excess fat
3 tablespoons catsup
1 tablespoon minced onion
1 teaspoon Worcestershire sauce
1/4 teaspoon dry mustard
1/4 teaspoon paprika
1/2 teaspoon salt
1 tablespoon vegetable oil
1 cup water

- Stir together the catsup, onion, Worcestershire sauce, mustard, paprika and salt.
- Spread mixture over chops. Place chops in a glass or ceramic dish, cover and chill several hours or overnight.
- Drain chops, reserving marinade.
- Heat a skillet, add oil, swirl to coat pan bottom.
- Brown chops on both sides. Put in a baking dish; add any remaining marinade and the cup of water. Cover dish.
- Heat oven to 375° and bake chops for 45 minutes, or until tender when pierced with tip of a knife.

Crisp Roast Potatoes

Serves 4

Everyone likes this guilt-free version of French fries.

4 large potatoes, peeled
2 quarts water
1 teaspoon salt
2 tablespoons vegetable oil
1/2 teaspoon paprika
nonstick cooking spray

* Bring 2 quarts of water to a boil, add salt.
* Slice potatoes lengthwise into 6 or 8 wedges each. Drop potatoes into boiling water; cook for 10 minutes; drain. Heat oven to 375°.
* Spray baking pan, arrange wedges in a single layer, drizzle on oil.
* Bake for 15 minutes; turn wedges over; sprinkle with paprika.
* Bake an additional 10 to 15 minutes until golden in color.

Maple Glazed Carrots

Serves 4

Carrots are a colorful and nutritious vegetable, inexpensive, and easy to keep on hand; there's a variety of ways to fix them.

2 tablespoons butter or margarine
2 tablespoons chopped onion
4 long carrots, thinly sliced (about 2 cups)
1/2 teaspoon salt
1/4 cup hot water
1 tablespoon maple syrup

* Melt the butter or margarine in a saucepan. Add the chopped onion and cook 2 minutes to soften.
* Add carrots, salt and water, cover the pan and cook over very low heat 20 to 25 minutes, until carrots are tender. Add more water during cooking if necessary. Or microwave 10-12 minutes.
* Place in a serving dish. Drizzle the maple syrup over the top.

Coleslaw with Yogurt Dressing

Serves 4

A crunchy and colorful salad that can be made ahead.

4 cups green cabbage, shredded
1/2 teaspoon salt
2 green onions, sliced thinly
1 medium-size carrot, shredded
1/3 cup plain low fat yogurt
1/3 cup light mayonnaise
1 tablespoon apple cider vinegar
1 teaspoon sugar
1/2 teaspoon salt

- Sprinkle salt on shredded cabbage and let stand 30 minutes.
- Stir in onions and carrots.
- Mix remaining ingredients in a small bowl for the dressing.
- Toss cabbage with the dressing. Mix well.
- Taste salad; add a little salt if needed.
- Chill 1 hour or longer. Toss well just before serving.

Helpful Hint

For ease in slicing green onions, first cut the onion lengthwise; then the crosswise slices will fall apart.

Seeded Rye Rolls

Makes 12 rolls

Crusty outsides and tender dark insides make these little rolls a dinner treat. Seeds add nutritional value, flavor and crunch.

1 tablespoon quick-acting yeast
1 tablespoon molasses
1 cup warm water, divided
2 tablespoons vegetable oil
1 cup unbleached white flour
1 cup rye flour
1 cup whole wheat flour
1/2 teaspoon salt
1 tablespoon caraway seeds
1 tablespoon sesame seeds

- Place yeast, molasses and 1/4 cup warm water in a bowl and let stand for 5 minutes until foamy.

- Stir in remaining water, oil, flours, salt and seeds.

- Turn out on a floured surface and knead 5 minutes, working in more flour if needed, until smooth and elastic.

- Lightly oil a large bowl, put dough in, and turn to coat it with oil. Cover bowl and keep warm until dough rises to double in bulk, about 1 to 2 hours.

- Spray a large baking sheet with nonstick cooking spray. Punch dough down; shape into 12 rounded balls. Place on sheet. Cover lightly with a towel.

- Let rise 40 minutes in a warm place.

- Heat oven to 375°. Bake rolls 20 to 25 minutes.

- Transfer rolls to a rack to cool. Serve warm.

Helpful Hint

Seeds contain volatile oils, so keep them in tightly covered jars in the refrigerator. They will remain fresh for months.

Lemon Squares
Serves 6

Sweet and tangy, this delectable dessert can be made ahead.

1 cup unbleached white flour
1/4 cup powdered sugar
1 stick butter or margarine, softened
2 eggs, well beaten
1 cup sugar
1/2 teaspoon baking powder
2 tablespoons fresh lemon juice
1 tablespoon powdered sugar for garnish

- Heat oven to 325° and set out an 8 x 8-inch pan.
- Stir the flour and powdered sugar together, cream in the butter. Pat this mixture evenly in the bottom of the pan.
- Bake for 20 minutes. Remove pan to a heat-proof surface to add filling.
- Raise oven temperature to 350°.
- Whisk together the beaten eggs, sugar, baking powder and lemon juice. The filling will be runny. Pour it into the crust.
- Return pan to hot oven and bake for 25 minutes.
- Remove from oven and cool.
- Just before serving, sift powdered sugar over the top. Cut into 6 squares and place each square on a dessert plate. These are generous servings; you may wish to cut this dessert into 9 squares.

Chicken Tetrazzini
Baby Peas with Mint
Garlic Toasts
Green Salad with Herb Dressing
French Apple Cake

Chicken Tetrazzini

Serves 4 to 6

Everyone likes pasta, and it's especially good in this dish, where a rich chickeny sauce sparkles with red and green peppers.

Preparing the chicken:

2 split chicken breasts (1 pound)
4 cups water
1 carrot, cut in large chunks
1 onion, cut in large chunks
1 rib celery, cut in 4 pieces
2 sprigs parsley
1 bay leaf
1/2 teaspoon salt

- Place chicken, water, vegetables and salt in a large kettle.
- Cover. Bring to a simmer and cook 40 to 45 minutes, until the chicken is tender when pierced with the tip of a knife.
- Set aside and let chicken cool in the broth.
- When cool, remove the skin and bones; cut chicken into two-inch pieces; keep covered in a 2-quart bowl.
- Strain the broth into a quart measure and reserve.

Preparing the sauce:

3 tablespoons butter or margarine
1 medium onion, chopped small
1 sweet green pepper, diced small
1 sweet red pepper, diced small
1/4 cup flour
2 cups chicken broth
1 cup milk
1 teaspoon Worcestershire sauce
1/2 to 1 teaspoon Tabasco sauce
1/2 teaspoon salt
1/4 teaspoon black pepper
2 tablespoons grated Parmesan cheese

- Melt butter or margarine in a 2-quart saucepan.
- Add onion and peppers; cook over medium low heat until soft.
- Sprinkle with the flour; stir and cook a few minutes.
- Slowly add the broth, whisking. Add the milk. Cook, stirring occasionally, until thickened; stir in seasonings and cheese.
- Last, add the chicken pieces. This can be done to here. Cool, cover
and refrigerate. Heat sauce before adding pasta.

Preparing the pasta:

1 pound thin spaghetti
1 teaspoon salt

- Bring 4 quarts of water to a boil in a large pan.
- Add salt and spaghetti. Boil, uncovered, stirring once or twice. Test a strand after 5 minutes to check doneness. Continue testing until pasta is tender but firm. Drain.
- Toss hot pasta with chicken and sauce. Serve hot.
- If desired, pass a bowl of grated Parmesan cheese.

Baby Peas with Mint

Serves 4

A caterer friend of mine doesn't cook frozen peas at all; she puts them in a pan, pours boiling water over them, drains and serves.

1 package (10 oz.) frozen baby peas, thawed
1/4 cup boiling water
1 sprig fresh mint, or 1 teaspoon dried, minced
1/4 teaspoon sugar
pinch of salt
extra fresh mint for garnish (optional)

- Bring water to a boil; add sugar, salt and mint.
- Drop in peas; stir once or twice; cook only until hot.
- Drain. Garnish with sprigs of fresh mint if desired.

Garlic Toasts

Serves 4 to 6

Leftover toasts can be cut into cubes and used for croutons.

1 loaf French bread
3 tablespoons butter or margarine, softened
4 cloves garlic, peeled, sliced

- Slice bread in half the long way, cut each half into 4 pieces.
- Mash butter or margarine and garlic together.
- Spread bread lightly with garlic mixture. Arrange pieces on baking sheet.
- Heat broiler. Place baking sheet 5 inches from heat and broil about 2 minutes until tops begin to brown.
- Place garlic toasts in a napkin-lined basket to serve.
- Bread can be cut and spread several hours in advance; cover with a tray until time to toast.

Green Salad

Serves 4

Today's produce markets offer a marvelous array of lettuces for our dining pleasure. Choose a variety for contrasts in texture.

5 cups torn leaf, romaine, Boston or Bibb lettuce
2 large sprigs parsley, minced
2 green onions, thinly sliced

- Wash lettuce leaves; place in a salad spinner or towel to dry. Tear into bite-size pieces. Keep wrapped and chilled until serving time.
- Shake up dressing just before tossing with the greens.
- Serve in a wooden or glass salad bowl or on salad plates.

Herb Dressing

Makes about 1/4 cup

This is so simple to make, but makes a salad taste so good.

1/4 teaspoon dry mustard
1/2 teaspoon salt
1 teaspoon dried basil
1 teaspoon dried oregano
1 tablespoon water
1 tablespoon white vinegar
2 tablespoons olive oil

- Measure the herbs , water and vinegar into a small glass jar and shake well; add oil last and shake again.
- Just before serving the salad, toss the greens together with the dressing, tossing well so greens glisten.

French Apple Cake

Serves 6

This tender, moist cake is easy to make and delightful to eat. Serve it warm from the oven, or make ahead and serve cold.

1 egg, beaten
1/4 cup water
3/4 cup sugar
1 teaspoon vanilla extract
1 cup unbleached white flour
1 teaspoon baking powder
Pinch of salt
3 red or yellow apples, peeled and diced
1/2 cup walnuts, chopped, toasted
Powdered sugar (optional)

- Heat oven to 350°. Lightly oil an 8 x 8-inch pan.

- Mix in a 2-quart bowl the beaten egg, water, sugar and vanilla.

- Stir in the flour, baking powder, salt, apples and walnuts.

- Spoon the batter into the pan; bake for 30-35 minutes.

- Remove and cool cake. Cut into 6 pieces. Just before serving, dust top of cake with sifted powdered sugar, if desired.

Helpful Hint

Nuts are more flavorful if toasted just before using. Toast in a dry skillet, shaking pan for a few minutes; or in a microwave by spreading nuts on a plate and toasting for 1 or 2 minutes, checking so they do not scorch; or bake at 350° for 5 to 10 minutes.

Cheese Strata Romanoff
Lemon Broccoli
Baked Tomato Halves
Whole Wheat Honey Rolls
Strawberry Meringue Tarts

Cheese Strata Romanoff

Serves 6

This classic dish must be made ahead, either the night before or several hours before serving.

8 slices day-old bread
2 tablespoons butter or margarine
12 ounces cheddar cheese, shredded
3 eggs, slightly beaten
1 1/2 cups milk
1/2 teaspoon brown sugar
1/2 teaspoon dry mustard
1/2 teaspoon salt
1 teaspoon Worcestershire sauce
1/8 teaspoon cayenne pepper

- Butter a shallow baking dish, approximately 7 x 10-inches.
- Trim crusts from bread; cut each slice in half. Spread butter or margarine on slices and arrange half on bottom of pan.
- Sprinkle bread with half the cheese. Top with rest of bread and cheese.
- Whisk eggs, milk and seasonings. Pour over bread.
- Cover and chill for 6 hours or overnight.
- Two hours before serving, take from refrigerator and let stand for 60 minutes at room temperature.
- Heat oven to 325°.
- Set dish into a larger shallow pan and put 1/2 inch of cold water in outer pan. Set in oven and bake 1 hour.
- Cut into squares and serve warm.

Lemon Broccoli

Serves 4

For broccoli that everyone will love, choose young, dark green broccoli with tight florets (the freshest) and do not overcook this great vegetable.

1 small head broccoli (3/4 to 1 pound)
1/2 teaspoon salt
2 tablespoons butter or margarine
2 tablespoons lemon juice
Dash of black pepper

- Cut broccoli tops into florets about 3 inches long.
- Peel the stems, cut in half lengthwise, and slice 1/2 inch thick on the diagonal.
- Heat 2 quarts of water to boiling; add salt and broccoli stems.
- Cook for about 2 minutes; add florets and cook one more minute. Begin to test for doneness; it should be slightly tender but still crisp. Drain.
- Place broccoli in dish. Melt butter or margarine, add lemon juice, and pour over broccoli. Add pepper and serve.

Baked Tomato Halves

Serves 4

A wonderful way to enjoy this vegetable when it's in season.

4 medium-size tomatoes
1/2 cup dry bread crumbs
1 tablespoon Parmesan cheese
Salt, pepper, paprika

- Heat oven to 325° and lightly oil a baking pan.
- Cut tomatoes in half horizontally, place halves on baking pan.
- Combine crumbs with cheese, divide onto top of tomato halves, and sprinkle each with salt, pepper and paprika.
- Bake for 20 to 25 minutes until heated through.

Whole Wheat Honey Rolls

Makes 12 rolls

The combination of whole wheat and unbleached white flours makes rolls that are light, luscious, and healthful.

2 teaspoons quick-acting yeast
1 cup warm water
2 tablespoons honey
1 tablespoon oil
1/2 teaspoon salt
1 1/2 cups whole wheat flour
1 1/2 cups unbleached white flour
2 tablespoons melted butter for dipping

- Stir together yeast, water and honey. Let stand 5 minutes.
- Stir in oil, salt and most of the flour. Turn out on a lightly floured work surface and knead for 5 to 10 minutes, until dough is smooth and elastic, adding more flour if needed.
- Place in a lightly oiled bowl and turn to coat dough. Cover with a kitchen towel.
- Let rise in a warm place until double, about 1 hour.
- Punch dough down and divide into 12 balls. Lightly oil muffin tins.
- Break each ball into 3 pieces; roll each piece into a little ball and dip it in the melted butter. Place 3 balls in each muffin tin.
- Cover and let rise 40 to 50 minutes. If it is a warm day, allow less time for the second rising.
- Heat oven to 375°, bake rolls 18 to 20 minutes, until golden. Oven temperatures vary, so check after 15 minutes. Rolls can be made ahead, cooled, and kept in refrigerator in a zipped bag. Just before serving , put in brown paper bag, sprinkle the bag with water and reheat rolls in the oven for 10 to 15 minutes.

Helpful Hint

If you dip measuring spoon in oil before measuring honey, the honey will slide right off the spoon.

Strawberry Meringue Tarts

Serves 4

Shells can be made ahead and stored in an airtight tin so they remain crisp and dry. Berries can be fixed ahead, too.

Meringue Shells:

2 egg whites
1/2 teaspoon vinegar
1/2 cup sugar
1 teaspoon vanilla extract

- Beat the egg whites until frothy. Add the vinegar and beat in the sugar, a little at a time. Add vanilla, beat until stiff.
- Fit a large piece of parchment or brown paper onto a cookie sheet. Draw four circles 4 inches in diameter on the paper, sketching around an inverted bowl.
- Spoon meringue into the circles, shaping shells.
- Heat oven to 250° and bake shells for 1 hour. Turn off oven, and leave shells in the oven for 1 hour to dry completely.
- Lift each shell carefully off the paper and store in an airtight tin.

Filling:

1 pint strawberries
1/4 cup sugar or to taste
Whipped cream or whipped topping

- Rinse berries. Cut up and stir in the sugar. Taste for sweetness, and add more sugar if needed. Chill berries until time to serve. Spoon berries into meringue shells and top with whipped cream or whipped topping.

Jambalaya with Ham and Rice
Cucumber and Lettuce Salad
Raspberry Jam Muffins
Apple Oatmeal Crisp

Jambalaya with Ham and Rice

Serves 4

A classic New Orleans dish made many different ways; some chefs add shrimp. Slow cooking blends the Cajun flavors.

2 tablespoons oil
2 large onions, diced
1 green pepper, chopped
2 ribs celery, diced
1/4 pound cooked ham, diced
4 chicken thighs
1 can (16 oz.) tomatoes, chopped
2 cups chicken broth
1 1/2 cups uncooked rice
1 teaspoon dried thyme
1/4 teaspoon paprika
1/8 teaspoon cayenne or black pepper
2 tablespoons parsley or chives for garnish

- Heat a dutch oven over medium heat; add oil.
- Add onion, pepper and celery. Cook 10 minutes, until soft.
- Add ham, chicken, tomatoes, and the broth.
- Cover pan. Cook 15 minutes. Add rice to pan; stir.
- Heat oven to 350° and bake 60-70 minutes, until rice is tender. Stir after 30 minutes.This can be done to here, cooled and put into a dish to refrigerate overnight. Reheat in a moderate oven.
- Before serving, sprinkle with chopped parsley or chives.

Cucumber and Lettuce Salad

Serves 4

A Danish friend fixes cucumbers this delicious way. They can be prepared hours ahead. and form the basis of a fat free salad.

1 medium-size cucumber
2 tablespoons chopped onion
1/2 teaspoon salt
1 teaspoon sugar
1 tablespoon vinegar
1 tablespoon water
3 cups lettuce, chopped or torn
1 tablespoon minced parsley

* Peel cucumber and slice thinly into a bowl, alternating with the chopped onions.
* Combine salt, sugar, vinegar and water in a small saucepan and bring to a boil. Stir to dissolve sugar.
* Stir the hot mixture into the cucumbers. Cover and chill for 2 hours.
* Just before serving, mix in the lettuce and parsley and toss.
* This is a pretty salad served in a glass bowl, or arranged on invidual salad plates.

Raspberry Jam Muffins

Makes 12 muffins

A delicious hot bread to serve with any meal. Good with other fruity preserves, too; try blueberry or strawberry.

1 cup unbleached white flour
1 cup whole wheat flour
1/3 cup sugar
2 1/2 teaspoons baking powder
1/4 teaspoon salt
1 egg, lightly beaten
1/4 cup vegetable oil
3/4 cup buttermilk
1/4 cup all-fruit raspberry preserves
1 tablespoon sugar for topping
1/4 teaspoon cinnamon

- Heat oven to 400°. Oil 12 muffin tins (2 1/2-inch size).

- Combine the flours, sugar, baking powder and salt. Mix well.

- Mix egg, oil and buttermilk. Stir into dry ingredients, being sure not to overmix. Try to combine wet and dry ingredients in 25 strokes.

- Spoon a tablespoonful of batter into each muffin cup. Put a teaspoon of preserves on each. Divide remaining batter into muffin tins on top of jam.

- Mix the sugar and cinnamon in a small bowl. Sprinkle this evenly on top of batter.

- Put in a hot oven and bake 20 minutes. Remove from pan and transfer to a napkin-lined basket to serve hot.

Apple Oatmeal Crisp

Serves 5 to 6

Adding orange juice and peel brightens the flavor of this classic dessert. Mince the zest before you squeeze the orange for juice.

5 to 6 medium-size apples, peeled and cored
1/3 cup orange juice
1/2 cup firmly packed brown sugar, divided
3 tablespoons butter or margarine
1/3 cup unbleached white flour
3/4 cup old-fashioned or quick-cooking oatmeal
1 tablespoon minced orange zest
1/2 teaspoon cinnamon
nonstick cooking spray for pan

- Heat oven to 350° and lightly spray 10 x 8 x 2-inch pan.
- Slice the peeled apples into the pan.
- Combine orange juice with 2 tablespoons of brown sugar and pour over the apples.
- Cream butter with the remaining sugar.
- Add flour, oatmeal, minced orange zest and cinnamon; mix until crumbly for topping.
- Sprinkle topping mixture over apples.
- Bake for 45 to 50 minutes, until apples are tender when pierced with tip of a knife. Serve warm or cold.

Helpful Hint

For orange zest, use a vegetable peeler to peel thin slices of orange skin, then chop it very small with a sharp knife. Avoid the white pith, as it is bitter.

Golden Mediterranean Vegetable Stew
Fluffy Couscous
Spring Salad with French Dressing
Orange Bowknot Rolls
Chocolate Mint Squares

Golden Mediterranean Vegetable Stew

Serves 4 to 5

Brimming with flavors to excite the palate, this is a favorite. It's even better the second day when flavors have mellowed.

2 tablespoons olive oil
2 cups thinly sliced onions
1 green or red pepper, cut in thin strips
1 tablespoon minced ginger root
1/2 teaspoon salt
1 teaspoon turmeric
1/2 teaspoon coriander
1/2 teaspoon dried oregano
1/4 teaspoon crushed red pepper flakes (optional)
1 can (16-oz.) garbanzo beans, drained
1 can (15-oz.) tomatoes, coarsely chopped
1/4 cup golden raisins

- Heat a large skillet or wok and swirl oil around to coat sides.
- Fry onions 5 minutes; add peppers, ginger and seasonings.
- Fry 5 minutes until soft; add beans, tomatoes and raisins.
- Cover the pan, bring to a simmer, and simmer over low heat for 20 minutes, stir once or twice.
- Serve with couscous, cooked rice or hot boiled potatoes.

Fluffy Couscous

Serves 4

Couscous is typical of Middle Eastern cuisine. It is a refined grain product made by extracting the heart of the wheat kernel (semolina). It is precooked, a quick, delicious, yellow grain.

1 1/2 cups vegetable broth
1 cup couscous

- Bring broth to a boil in a small pan.
- Stir couscous into broth; cover pan; remove from heat. Let stand 20 minutes; fluff with a fork. This makes about 2 1/2 cups.

Vegetable Broth

This will keep in a covered jar in the refrigerator for several days, or will keep for 3 months in a freezer.

1 medium-size onion, peeled
1 carrot, cut in chunks
3 cloves garlic
1 rib celery, with leaves, cut up
6 sprigs of parsley
5 cups cold water
1/2 teaspoon salt

- Cut onion into quarters. Smash the garlic; remove peel.
- Place vegetables in a 2-quart pan, add the parsley, water and 1/2 teaspoon salt. Bring to a boil, reduce heat and simmer for 30 minutes with a cover not quite all the way on the pan.
- Strain broth, pressing vegetables into the strainer to extract liquid. Taste and add a little more salt if needed. This makes about one quart.

Spring Salad
Serves 4

A simple crisp salad is a refreshing contrast to a piquant main dish. Red radishes add a color accent.

5 cups lettuce or salad greens, washed and dried
4 to 6 radishes, washed, sliced thinly
2 green onions, sliced thinly

French Dressing

This is enough dressing for two big salads.

1/4 teaspoon salt
1/4 teaspoon paprika
1/4 teaspoon sugar
3 tablespoons white vinegar
6 tablespoons olive oil

- Combine seasonings with vinegar in a small jar. Cover jar and shake well. Add oil; shake again. Makes 1/2 cup dressing.
- Pour half the dressing over well washed and dried leaves
  of lettuce, romaine or other salad greens and toss well. Toss
  again with sliced radishes and onions.
- Save remaining dressing for another salad, but use within a day or two to maintain a fresh taste.

Orange Bowknot Rolls

makes 24

This fragrant, light little roll will be welcome at any meal. Grate the rind from an orange before you cut it for juice.

2 teaspoons quick-acting yeast
2 tablespoons sugar
1/2 cup warm water
2 tablespoons vegetable oil
1/2 cup orange juice
2 tablespoons grated orange peel
2 cups unbleached white flour
1 to 1 1/2 cups whole wheat flour
1/2 teaspoon salt

- Combine yeast, sugar and 1/2 cup warm water in a bowl and let stand 5 minutes, until foamy.
- Add oil, juice, orange peel, white flour, and salt; stir well.
- Beat in enough flour to make a soft dough that holds together in a ball; beating very well.
- Cover dough and let rise in a warm place until double in bulk.
- Spray a large baking sheet wih nonstick cooking oil spray.
- Punch down dough and roll out into a rectangle about 1/2 inch thick. Cut into strips about 1/2 inch wide. Tie each in a knot.
- Place rolls on baking sheet, tucking ends under. Cover; let rise 30 to 40 minutes until almost double in size.
- Heat oven to 400° and bake rolls 15 minutes.
- While rolls are warm, spread with a thin glaze.

Orange Glaze

1 cup powdered sugar
1 teaspoon grated orange peel
1 to 2 tablespoons orange juice

- Combine ingredients. Mixture will be thin. Spoon over rolls.

Chocolate Mint Squares

makes 9 squares

These are chewy and moist. Almonds add crunch and nutrition.

2 eggs, slightly beaten
1 cup sugar
1/4 cup vegetable oil
1/3 cup unsweetened cocoa powder
1/2 cup unbleached white flour
1/2 teaspoon peppermint extract
1/2 cup almonds, slivered (optional)

- Heat oven to 350°. Lightly oil an 8 x 8-inch pan.
- Put sliced almonds on a pie plate and roast for 6 to 8 minutes. Remove; cool. Save a few slivers to garnish top, if desired.
- Beat eggs with a whisk; beat in sugar, oil, cocoa and flour.
- Stir in peppermint extract and almonds.
- Pour into prepared pan; bake 25 minutes. Cool.
- Frost, if desired. Cut into 9 squares to serve.

Chocolate Frosting

2 tablespoons butter or margarine
1/4 cup unsweetened cocoa powder
1 teaspoon vanilla extract
1 cup powdered sugar
1 to 2 tablespoons strong coffee or water

- Soften butter or margarine; stir in cocoa and vanilla.
- Stir in powdered sugar and add 1 tablespoon liquid.
- Mix until frosting is smooth and of spreading consistency.
- If too stiff, add a teaspoon or two of coffee or water.
- Spread frosting on top of squares. If desired, press a few almond slivers on top of each square.

Shrimp Fettuccine
Spinach Orange Salad
Ginger Dressing
Herbed Pita Bread Triangles
Date Walnut Cake

Shrimp Fettuccine

Serves 4

An elegant entree with savory Mediterranean flavors.

3/4 pound fresh or frozen shrimp
1 (16-oz.) package fettuccine
1 teaspoon salt
2 tablespoons olive oil
3 cloves garlic, peeled and sliced
1/4 teaspoon red pepper flakes
1 large ripe tomato, diced
1 cup frozen green peas
1/4 cup reserved pasta water
grated Parmesan cheese (optional)

- Drop shrimp into a large pot of boiling water; cook a few minutes, watching carefully, until they just begin to turn pink. Drain and rinse with cold water.
- Remove shells. With a sharp knife, make a shallow slit down the center of the backs. Scrape out the black vein, if any. Rinse. Cut each shrimp into several pieces. These can be prepared the day before. Store in covered bowl in refrigerator.
- Bring 4 quarts of water to a boil. Add pasta and salt. Cook the fettuccine until al dente, about 10 minutes. Save some cooking water when you drain the pasta; keep pasta warm.
- Heat a large skillet or wok, add oil. When oil is hot, add shrimp and red pepper flakes. Cook a minute, stir in sliced garlic.
- Add tomato, peas and 1/4 cup pasta water and cover pan.
- Cook 5 minutes, taste and add salt if needed. Toss with pasta.
- Pass grated Parmesan cheese if desired.

Spinach Orange Salad

Serves 4

Colorful and crisp with fresh garden spinach and a tangy, fruity dressing to add just before serving.

1/2 pound young spinach leaves
1/2 head lettuce or romaine
1 orange, peeled, thinly sliced
1/4 purple onion, thinly sliced

Wash lettuce and spinach well, cut off tough stems, dry.

Ginger Dressing

1 teaspoon grated fresh ginger root
2 tablespoons orange juice
2 tablespoons olive oil
2 teaspoons white vinegar
1 teaspoon soy sauce

• Measure ingredients into a small jar and shake up.

Herbed Pita Bread Triangles

Serves 4

An easy little hot bread to prepare. Some stores carry whole wheat, onion, sesame, or garlic flavored pitas, so you can try different flavors. Keep pita breads on hand in the freezer.

4 pita breads
1 tablespoon olive oil
1 teaspoon dried oregano
1 teaspoon dried basil
1 clove garlic, sliced

• Heat oven to 350°. Combine oil, herbs and garlic in a small pan and warm over low heat.

• Brush both sides of each pita with mixture; place on baking sheet. Bake 4 to 5 minutes, until hot but not too crisp.

• Cut each pita in quarters before serving.

Date Walnut Cake

Serves 6 to 9

This is an old-time dessert that tastes good today. It can be glamorized by serving with a dollop of whipped cream.

1 cup pitted dates, cut up
1 cup boiling water
1 cup sugar
1/4 cup vegetable oil
1 egg, slightly beaten
1 teaspoon vanilla extract
1 1/2 cups unbleached white flour
1 teaspoon baking soda
1/2 teaspoon salt
1 tablespoon unsweetend cocoa powder
1/2 cup chopped walnuts, toasted
Powdered sugar for topping

- Heat oven to 350°. Lightly oil an 8 x 8-inch pan.
- Pour boiling water over dates and let stand 5 minutes.
- Spread chopped walnuts on a pie tin and toast in oven for 6 to 8 minutes. Cool.
- Mix together sugar, oil, egg, and vanilla; add dates in water.
- Sift together the flour, soda, salt and cocoa.
- Mix wet and dry ingredients; stir in toasted walnuts.
- Spoon batter into pan. Bake 45 minutes. Cool.
- Sprinkle top of cake with powdered sugar.
- Cut into 6 large squares or 9 medium-size squares to serve.

Helpful Hint

When cutting dates, dip your knife or kitchen scissors into a cup of hot water to make the job easier.

Chicken Almond Rice Casserole
Grapefruit and Avocado Salad
Lemon Honey Dressing
Dilly Cheese Rolls
Blueberry Buckle

Chicken Almond Rice Casserole

Serves 4 to 6

The friend who gave me this recipe cooks a whole chicken for it. I poach a pound of split chicken breasts or use leftover turkey.

2 cups cooked chicken or turkey,
    boned and diced into 1-inch chunks
2 1/2 cups cooked rice (1 cup raw)
1/4 cup onion, chopped very fine
2 cups celery, diced small
1 can mushroom soup, undiluted
1/2 cup light mayonnaise

- Lightly butter a 2-quart shallow oval or oblong baking dish.
- Mix soup and mayonnaise.
- Mix all ingredients together and place in dish.
- This can be prepared the day before; cover and chill. Bring to room temperature and add the topping just before baking.

Topping:

1 cup crushed cornflakes
1/3 cup toasted slivered almonds
3 tablespoons melted butter or margarine

- Heat oven to 350°. Have casserole at room temperature.
- Mix topping ingredients and sprinkle over casserole.
- Bake 30 to 40 minutes until bubbling.

Grapefruit and Avocado Salad

Serves 4

A pretty salad to arrange on individual chilled salad plates or to simply toss with dressing in a glass or pottery bowl.

1 head Bibb or Boston lettuce
1 large grapefruit
1 avocado
A few thin slices of mild purple onion

- Wash the lettuce; dry well on a towel. Tear into smaller pieces.
- Peel and slice the grapefruit; discard seeds and membranes.
- Peel avocado just before serving. Make dressing ahead.
- At serving time, toss the torn lettuce, grapefruit and onion with Lemon Honey Dressing. Slice the avocado into salad last.

Lemon Honey Dressing

This light and refreshing dressing goes great with all different kinds of greens, and has become a family favorite.

2 tablespoons lemon juice
1 teaspoon minced lemon rind or zest
2 teaspoons honey
1/8 teaspoon dry mustard
1/4 teaspoon paprika
1/4 teaspoon salt
1/4 cup vegetable oil

- Peel a few thin strips of yellow rind from the lemon before squeezing for juice. Mince the strips of lemon rind for zest.
- Measure lemon juice, rind, and seasonings into a small bowl; whisk well. Whisk in honey, then mix in oil last. Chill.
- Stir dressing well just before using.

Dilly Cheese Rolls

Makes 12

These delectable little breads have a crusty outside, moist savory inside, and are easy to make.

> 2 teaspoons quick-acting yeast
> 1/4 cup warm water
> 1 tablespoon sugar
> 1 cup small curd cottage cheese, warmed
> 1 egg
> 1 tablespoon oil
> 1 tablespoon dried onion flakes
> 2 teaspoons dried dill weed
> 1/2 teaspoon salt
> 2 1/2 cups unbleached white flour

- Combine the yeast, warm water and sugar and let stand 5 minutes until foamy.

- Stir in remaining ingredients, mixing well. Cover and let stand for 1 hour, until double in bulk.

- Punch dough down. Spray bottoms and sides of 12 muffin tins with non stick cooking spray, or oil tins well.

- Spoon dough evenly into the 12 tins.

- Let rise again until double in bulk, about 40 minutes.

- Heat oven to 375°. Bake rolls 15 to 20 minutes, until lightly browned on top.

- Run a sharp knife around edge of each roll to loosen, put rolls into a napkin-lined basket to serve warm. Leftover rolls are delicious the next day if sliced in half and toasted.

Blueberry Buckle

Serves 6 to 9

A favorite dessert to make again and again when blueberries are in season.

1/4 cup butter or margarine
3/4 cup sugar
1 egg
1 teaspoon vanilla extract
1/2 cup milk
2 cups flour
2 teaspoons baking powder
1/2 teaspoon salt
1 1/2 cups blueberries

- Heat oven to 375°. Lightly oil an 8 x 8-inch pan.
- Rinse and pick over blueberries; drain well.
- Cream butter or margarine with the sugar; add egg and vanilla.
- Stir in milk; add flour, baking powder and salt. Mix well.
- Stir in blueberries. Pour into prepared baking dish.
- Sprinkle streusel mixture over batter.

Streusel Topping:

1/2 cup sugar
1/2 cup flour
1/2 teaspoon cinnamon
1/4 cup butter or margarine, softened

- Mix until crumbly with a pastry blender. Sprinkle on batter.
- Bake at 375° for 45 minutes.
- Serve warm or cool. Cut into 6 or 9 squares to serve.

Tamale Pie
Cauliflower with Crumb Topping
Two-Green Salad with Apple
Chocolate Pudding Cake

Tamale Pie

Serves 6

South-of-the-border flavors mingle in this tantalizing dish.

3 cups vegetable broth
1 teaspoon salt
1 cup yellow cornmeal
1/2 pound lean ground beef
1 large onion, chopped small
1 large green pepper, diced
2 teaspoons chili powder
1 teaspoon ground cumin
2 cups tomatoes (15 oz. can) chopped
2 cups (16 oz. can) kidney or pinto beans
Salt and pepper to taste
1/2 cup shredded cheese (optional)

- Bring broth to a boil in top of a double boiler; add salt.

- Slowly whisk in the cornmeal, stirring constantly in one direction until thick. Cover and cook over low heat 20 minutes.

- In a skillet, cook ground beef over medium-high heat 5 minutes. Add onion and green pepper; cook 5 minutes more. Stir in seasonings. Add tomatoes and beans.

- Oil a 2-quart casserole; spread half the cornmeal mush for a bottom layer. Spoon in the beef filling. Spread remaining mush on top. If desired, sprinkle with 1/2 cup shredded cheese.

- *Casserole can be made ahead to here.Cover and chill. Bring to room temperature before baking.*

- Heat oven to 350° and bake 50 to 60 minutes.

Cauliflower with Crumb Topping

Serves 4

This looks good and tastes good. You can whiz a slice of bread in the blender to make soft crumbs.

1 medium-size cauliflower
1 teaspoon vinegar
1/2 cup soft bread crumbs
1 tablespoon olive oil

- Remove outside leaves from cauliflower. Break into flowers, and discard core. Submerge in cold water to rinse. Drain.
- Bring 2 quarts water to a boil; add vinegar and cauliflower.
- Cook until tender, 10 to 15 minutes. Drain, keep warm.
- Heat oil in a small pan, stir fry the crumbs until lightly brown.
- Place cauliflower in a serving bowl, top with crumbs.

Helpful Hint

Avoid odors when cooking cauliflower by adding a slice of bread to the cooking water. Discard bread with water.

Two-Green Salad with Apple

Serves 4

This salad's light and dark greens are complemented by the red of an apple. It's crisp and refreshing. If I feel extravagant, I toss in a handful of toasted walnuts.

1/2 pound green leaf lettuce
1/2 pound young spinach leaves
2 green onions, sliced 1/4 inch thick
1 small red apple
1/4 teaspoon salt
1/8 teaspoon black pepper
1/4 teaspoon dry mustard
2 tablespoons apple cider vinegar
4 tablespoons olive oil

- Wash lettuce and spinach; dry on a towel. Slice onions.
- Remove tough stems from spinach and discard.
- Tear lettuce and spinach into bite size pieces; keep cool.
- In bottom of a glass salad bowl, mix seasonings and vinegar.
- Stir in the olive oil; cover dressing with a saucer. Set aside.
- Just before serving, stir the dressing; add greens and onion.
- Slice apple thinly into the greens.
- Toss greens and apple well to coat with dressing.

Chocolate Pudding Cake

Serves 4 to 6

This recipe will satisfy any chocolate lover. It makes its own topping as it bakes, so it needs no icing. Serve it warm.

1 cup unbleached white flour
3/4 cup sugar
3 tablespoons unsweetened cocoa powder
2 teaspoons baking powder
1/2 teaspoon salt
2 tablespoons vegetable oil
1/2 cup milk
1 teaspoon vanilla extract

- Heat oven to 350°. Lightly oil an 8 x 8-inch baking pan.
- Whisk the dry ingredients together, then add liquids, stirring until smooth. Pour into prepared baking pan.
- In a separate bowl, mix:

  3/4 cup brown sugar, firmly packed
  1/4 cup unsweetened cocoa powder
- Sprinkle this sugar mixture over top of batter. Pour on:

  1 3/4 cup boiling water
- Bake 45 minutes. Serve warm.

Spinach-Stuffed Shells
Williamsburg Cabbage Salad
Breadsticks with Sesame Seeds
Magic Coconut Pie

Spinach-Stuffed Shells

Serves 4

Some shells may break, but there's no rule against stuffing broken shells and tucking them into the dish.

4 ounces jumbo pasta shells
1 package (10 oz.) frozen chopped spinach
2 tablespoons olive oil
1 small onion, finely chopped
16 ounces ricotta or low fat cottage cheese
2 tablespoons minced parsley
1 teaspoon dried oregano
1/2 teaspoon salt
1/4 teaspoon garlic powder
About 3 cups tomato sauce (see recipe)
2 tablespoons Parmesan cheese

- Cook shells according to package directions.
- Drain; add a little cold water to cool shells.
- Defrost and drain spinach . Squeeze out excess liquid.
- In a small pan heat olive oil and saute onion until soft.
- Mix onion with ricotta or cottage cheese, spinach, parsley, oregano, salt, garlic. Spoon filling into shells, handling gently.
- Put a third of the tomato sauce in bottom of a 9 x 9-inch pan.
- Set shells in pan. Pour stripes of the remaining sauce over the shells. Sprinkle with Parmesan cheese.
- Heat oven to 375° and bake 25 to 30 minutes.

Tomato Sauce

Makes about 3 cups

There is no need to buy an expensive sauce when this is so easy to make.

1 can (28 oz.) plum tomatoes, cut up
1 teaspoon dehydrated onion flakes
1/2 teaspoon dried basil
1/2 teaspoon dried oregano
1/2 teaspoon sugar

• Whiz all ingredients in blender. Taste and add a pinch of salt if needed.

Williamsburg Cabbage Salad

Serves 4

A colorful salad with a piquant, slightly sweet dressing.

3 cups shredded cabbage
1 rib celery, diced small
1 small onion, diced
1 medium carrot, grated
1 ripe tomato, chopped

• Combine vegetables in a bowl; cover and chill. Mix:

1/4 cup vegetable oil
2 tablespoons white vinegar
2 tablespoons sugar
1/2 teaspoon salt
1/2 teaspoon celery seeds (optional)

• One hour before serving, toss cabbage with dressing, cover and let stand to blend flavors. Chill. Stir well just before serving.

Breadsticks with Sesame Seeds

Makes 16 breadsticks

These can be made ahead and frozen for up to two months.

2 teaspoons quick-acting yeast
1 cup warm water, divided
1 teaspoon sugar
1 tablespoon vegetable oil
1 teaspoon salt
2 cups whole wheat flour
2 cups unbleached white flour, divided
2 tablespoons sesame seeds for topping

- In a large bowl, combine the yeast, 1/4 cup warm water, and the sugar. Let stand 5 minutes to get foamy.
- Add remaining water, oil and salt. Stir in whole wheat flour.
- Set half the white flour aside to work in while kneading and stir in remaining flour. Turn out onto a floured work surface.
- Knead 5 to 10 minutes, working in flour as needed, until dough is elastic and smooth.
- Place in an oiled bowl, turn to coat dough, cover, let rise until doubled in size, about 1 hour.
- Spray 10 x 15-inch baking sheet with nonstick cooking spray.
- Spread sesame seeds out on a piece of foil.
- Divide dough into 4 equal parts; divide each into 4 balls. Take one ball at a time and roll and stretch until it is 10 inches long.
- Roll strip in sesame seeds; place on baking sheet. Continue until 16 bread sticks are made.
- Let rise 20 minutes. Heat oven to 375°.
- Bake 20 to 25 minutes, until lightly browned.

Magic Coconut Pie

Serves 6 to 8

The magic is that this delicious pie makes its own crust and topping as it bakes. It takes only minutes to make in a blender.

2 cups milk
1/4 cup sugar
2 tablespoons melted butter or margarine
3 eggs
1/2 cup unbleached white flour
1 teaspoon vanilla extract
1 cup dried unsweetened coconut

- Heat oven to 350°. Lightly butter a 9-inch pie plate.

- Measure all ingredients into a blender. Cover and whiz.

- Pour mixture into the buttered pie plate.

- Bake for 45 minutes.

- Cool on a rack. Chill until serving time.

- Cut in wedges to serve.

- This can be made the day before; cover and keep refrigerated.

Individual Meat Loaves
Parsley Potatoes
Green Beans with Mushrooms
Buttermilk Biscuits
Chocolate Pecan Pie

Individual Meat Loaves

Serves 4 to 6

This recipe came from Lenny Angel, a leading caterer in San Antonio. Baked in a very hot oven, these are outstanding!

1 1/2 pounds ground beef
1 teaspoon salt
1/4 teaspoon pepper
2 tablespoons dried onion flakes (no substitutes)
1 egg
1 cup soft bread crumbs
1 can (8 oz.) tomato sauce

Topping Sauce:

1 can (8 oz.) tomato sauce
2 tablespoons brown sugar
2 tablespoons minced fresh parsley
1 teaspoon Worcestershire sauce
1/2 teaspoon salt, or to taste

- Heat oven to 450°. Set out a baking sheet with sides.
- Mix meat loaf ingredients and shape into 8 oval loaves.
- Place loaves on baking sheet.
- Bake 15 minutes. Remove from oven and pour off grease.
- Mix the ingredients for the topping sauce; taste to check salt.
- Spoon topping over the meat loaves.
- Return loaves to oven and bake 5 minutes more at high heat.
- Reduce heat to 350° and bake 10 minutes more. Transfer from pan to serving platter or individual plates.
- Leftover loaves are great cold, sliced for sandwiches.

Parsley Potatoes

Serves 4

Accent the naturally good flavor of young, new potatoes with fresh green parsley, or any other fresh herb.

8 to 12 small "new" potatoes (1 pound)
1/2 teaspoon salt
2 tablespoons butter or margarine, melted
2 tablespoons finely chopped parsley

- Scrub the potatoes well. If potatoes are not small, cut in half.
- Bring 2 quarts water to a boil; add salt and potatoes; cover.
- Cook until tender when pierced with tip of a knife, about 15 to 20 minutes.
- Drain potatoes into a colander that you have placed over your serving dish so that the cooking water will heat the dish. Watch out for overflow! Discard water and transfer potatoes to the dish.
- Add melted butter or margarine and stir gently to coat.
- Sprinkle with the parsley and serve at once.

Green Beans with Mushrooms

Serves 4

Don't overcook green beans. They should be tender but retain some crispness. If mushrooms are expensive, substitute a thinly sliced white onion in this dish.

1 (10-oz.) package French-cut green beans
1/4 pound fresh mushrooms
1 tablespoon butter or margarine
1/2 teaspoon salt
1/4 teaspoon ground nutmeg

- Drop green beans into boiling water; cook 3 to 5 minutes. Drain. Keep warm.
- Rinse mushrooms, wipe clean and slice.
- Heat a small skillet; melt butter and stir fry mushrooms 3 to 5 minutes, until they begin to turn brown.
- Stir the drained beans into the mushrooms.
- Sprinkle with salt and nutmeg and serve hot.

Buttermilk Biscuits

Makes 15 biscuits

Bite into this tender, crusty little biscuit and enjoy the flavor and hearty goodness of whole wheat .

1 cup whole wheat flour
1 cup unbleached white flour
2 teaspoons baking powder
1/2 teaspoon baking soda
1 teaspoon salt
3/4 cup buttermilk
1/4 cup vegetable oil

- Heat oven to 425°.
- Lightly spray a baking sheet with nonstick cooking spray.
- Measure into a bowl the flours, baking powder, baking soda and salt. Stir to mix well.
- Stir in the buttermilk and oil, working in to form a soft dough.
- Knead a little with your hand so dough is well mixed.
- Pinch off 16 balls of dough and pat into rounds about 2 inches wide and 1/2 inch thick, placing each on the baking sheet.
- Bake for 12 to 14 minutes, until golden brown on top.
- Remove from oven and put biscuits in a napkin-lined basket.

Serve warm.

Helpful Hint

Biscuits bake more evenly on a baking sheet that
has no sides, as the hot air can circulate around them.

Chocolate Pecan Pie

Serves 8

This is a marvelously rich dessert to serve on a special occasion when no one is counting calories.

1 unbaked 9-inch pastry shell (page 145)
3 eggs
3/4 cup firmly packed brown sugar
1 cup light corn syrup
1 teaspoon vanilla extract
A pinch of salt
1 cup (6 oz.) chocolate chips
1 cup pecans, broken

* Heat oven to 400°. Place pecans on a baking sheet and toast for 3 to 4 minutes; cool.

* Have an unbaked pie shell ready.

* In a mixing bowl, beat eggs lightly and whisk in sugar and salt.

* Whisk in corn syrup and vanilla. Stir in chocolate chips and toasted pecans. Pour into unbaked shell.

* Bake 10 minutes at 400°. Reduce heat to 325° and continue baking 40 to 45 minutes, or until set. If crust is beginning to brown too early, remove pie from oven and cover crust with a strip of foil. Return pie to oven at once.

* When pie is set, a knife inserted in center will come out clean.

* Remove pie from oven and let cool.

* Pie can be made a day ahead; keep covered.

Broccoli Bisque
Focaccia with Onions and Walnuts
Greek Salad with Feta Cheese
Poppy Seed Loaf Cake

Broccoli Bisque

Serves 4

This recipe was given to me by a Swiss friend and is absolutely delicious served either hot or cold.

1 stalk broccoli (about 8 ounces)
1 onion, roughly cut
2 1/2 cups chicken or vegetable broth
1 teaspoon salt
1 teaspoon curry powder
1 tablespoon lemon juice
Chopped chives or green onion top for garnish

- Wash broccoli, cut off tough end, and peel stem.
- Finely chop the broccoli flowers and stem to make 2 cups.
- Combine in a 2-quart saucepan the broccoli, onion, broth, salt and curry powder. Cover pan, bring to a boil; reduce heat and simmer 10 minutes.
- Remove from heat and cool for 10 minutes.
- Add the lemon juice, and puree in a blender until smooth.
- Cover and chill if serving cold.
- Return to stove if serving hot; heat and ladle into soup bowls.
- Sprinkle with finely chopped chives or thinly sliced green onion top.

Focaccia with Onions and Walnuts

Serves 6 to 8

Pronounced foh-cah'-she-uh, it's an Italian flat bread baked with various toppings, like herbs, black olives, or vegetables.

2 teaspoons quick-acting yeast
1 cup warm water, divided
1 teaspoon sugar
2 tablespoons olive oil
1 cup whole wheat flour
2 1/2 to 3 cups unbleached white flour
1/2 teaspoon salt

* Combine yeast, 1/4 cup warm water and sugar in a large bowl and let stand 5 minutes, until foamy.

* Stir in remaining water, oil, and the flour. Add salt.

* Turn out on a lightly floured surface and knead for 5 minutes, adding more flour if needed, until dough is soft and elastic.

* Put dough in an oiled bowl; cover bowl with a kitchen towel.

* Keep in a warm place until double in size. Prepare topping.

Topping:

2 tablespoons olive oil
2 large onions, about 1 1/2 pounds, thinly sliced
1/2 teaspoon salt
1/2 cup walnuts, chopped

* Heat a large skillet; add oil, onions and salt. Cook over low heat for about an hour, until onions begin to caramelize. Stir from time to time, adding a few drops of water if too dry.

* Oil a 10 1/2 x 15-inch baking sheet with sides. Heat oven to 400°.

* Roll and stretch the dough to fit the pan. Using a fork, prick dough all over. This lets topping flavors seep through.

* Spread onions over top of dough, sprinkle with the walnuts.

* Place pan in oven; bake 25 minutes. Cut into 20 squares.

Greek Salad with Feta Cheese

Serves 4

The bountiful flavors of the Mediterranean merge in a big salad. A little creamy, tangy feta cheese adds an authentic touch.

4 to 5 cups lettuce, washed, dried, torn up
1 tomato, cut into wedges
1 small cucumber, thinly sliced
1/4 of a purple or red onion, diced small
1/4 to 1/2 cup feta cheese, crumbled (1 to 2 oz.)
1/4 cup black ripe olives, pitted, sliced (optional)

Dressing:

3 tablespoons olive oil
1 tablespoon red wine vinegar
1/2 teaspoon salt
1/2 teaspoon dried oregano
1/2 teaspoon dried basil

- Prepare vegetables. Cover and chill until serving time.
- Combine dressing ingredients in a small jar, shake well.
- Just before serving, toss lettuce and vegetables well with the dressing. Crumble the feta cheese on top.
- If desired, garnish with slices of black ripe olives.

Poppy Seed Loaf Cake

Makes 16 slices

This cake will keep for a week in the refrigerator, wrapped in foil.
An electric mixer or a food processor will whip it up quickly.

1/4 cup poppy seeds
1/2 cup evaporated milk
1/2 cup water
1/2 cup butter or margarine
1 1/2 cups sugar
2 eggs, lightly beaten
1/8 teaspoon salt
1 teaspoon vanilla extract
2 cups unbleached white flour
2 teaspoons baking powder
Powdered sugar to sprinkle on top of cake

- Combine milk and water and soak poppy seeds in this mixture for 1 hour.
- Heat oven to 350°. Spray 8 x 5-inch loaf pan with nonstick cooking spray.
- Cream the butter or margarine with the sugar.
- Beat in eggs, salt, vanilla, and the poppy seed mixture.
- Beat in flour and baking powder. Beat well.
- Pour batter into pan and bake for 55 to 60 minutes. When done, the top of the cake will spring back when touched lightly with a finger, and sides of cake will begin to pull away from the pan.
- Cool 10 minutes, turn out of pan. Sprinkle top with powdered sugar. When cake is cold, wrap in foil to keep fresh.

> **Szechwan Shrimp**
> **Lettuce Salad with Green Dressing**
> **Herbed French Bread**
> **Lemon Pudding Cakes**

Szechwan Shrimp

Serves 4

Have everything ready for this delectable combination, and stir-fry it just before serving. Buy shrimp when it's on special.

8 to12 ounces fresh or frozen shrimp
2 tablespoons vegetable oil, divided
1 red pepper, cut in thin 2-inch strips
1 green pepper, cut in thin 2-inch strips
1 large onion, thinly sliced
2 teaspoons minced ginger root

Sauce:

1/4 cup chicken broth
2 tablespoons catsup
1 tablespoon soy sauce
1 teaspoon cornstarch
1/2 teaspoon sugar

- Mix sauce ingredients in a small bowl; set aside.
- Bring 3 quarts water to a boil; add shrimp; cook 3 minutes.
- Drain. Rinse in cold water, slip off shells and remove any black lines down the back. Cut each into 3 or 4 pieces. Set aside. Prepare shrimp and vegetables ahead, keep refrigerated.
- Heat a large skillet or wok, add 1 tablespoon of oil, swirl pan around to coat, add the vegetables and ginger root.
- Stir-fry 5 minutes until vegetables are tender but crisp.
- Remove vegetables from pan; put into a bowl.
- Add 1 tablespoon oil to pan and stir-fry shrimp 2 or 3 minutes; stir in the sauce; return vegetables to pan; stir all together.
- Serve with hot cooked white or brown rice.

Lettuce Salad with Green Dressing

Serves 4

The crisp cool greens of this salad provide a pleasing, subtle contrast in colors, flavors and textures.

5 cups washed leaf or Boston lettuce
2 tablespoons olive oil
1 tablespoon vinegar
2 tablespoons chopped green onions
2 tablespoons minced parsley
1/2 teaspoon salt
1/4 teaspoon dry mustard
1/8 teaspoon black pepper

- Wash lettuce; dry well on a kitchen towel.

- Tear lettuce into bite-size pieces. Keep covered, and store in the refrigerator until serving time.

- Stir together the oil, vinegar, salt, pepper and mustard or shake in a small jar. Add minced parsley and chopped onions.

- Toss dressing well with lettuce just before serving.

Herbed French Bread

Serves 4

Any leftover bread makes delicious croutons to save for salad or soup. Just cut bread into bite-size cubes and freeze in a plastic bag.

1 small loaf French bread
1/4 cup (1/2 stick) butter or margarine
2 tablespoons minced fresh parsley
1 large garlic clove, smashed, minced
1 teaspoon dried basil or dill weed

- Heat oven to 375°. Have baking pan and foil ready.
- Slice almost through bread at two-inch intervals, leaving bread attached at the bottom crust.
- Mix remaining ingredients and spread on bread slices. Place loaf on foil, leaving top exposed. Bake about 10 minutes.
- This may be prepared ahead and baked just before serving.

Lemon Pudding Cakes

Serves 6

Tangy and sweet, these little desserts are light and lovely. They may be made a day or even two days before serving.

3 eggs, separated
1 cup sugar
1/4 cup unbleached white flour
2 tablespoons melted butter or margarine
Grated rind of 1 lemon
1/4 cup lemon juice (about 1 1/2 lemons)
1 1/2 cups milk
Whipped cream or topping if desired

- Butter 6 ramekins or custard cups.
- Have a baking pan ready to set them in.
- Note: If you do not have individual ramekins or custard cups, this dessert can be made in a 9-inch pie pan. Set the pan into a larger pan of warm water to bake.
- Heat oven to 350°.
- Separate egg yolks and whites into 2 bowls.
- Beat yolks well and beat in sugar, then flour.
- Beat in lemon rind and juice, then add milk.
- Beat egg whites until stiff and fold into the batter.
- Pour into buttered ramekins. Pour warm water into the baking pan to 1/2 inch depth and set ramekins in the pan.
- Bake 45 minutes, until lightly browned on top.
- Cool. Serve with whipped cream, if desired. These can be served in the ramekin or unmolded onto a dessert plate.

Provençal Beans with Dill
Jalapeño Corn Muffins
Red and Yellow Tomato Salad
Pineapple Ice Box Dessert

Provençal Beans with Dill

Serves 4 to 5

An aromatic and flavorful dish, but inexpensive. Cooking beans from scratch takes time but saves money.

1 1/2 cups dried white lima beans
2 quarts boiling water
1 teaspoon salt
2 tablespoons olive oil
2 medium-size carrots, thinly sliced
2 ribs celery, thinly sliced
2 cloves garlic, minced
2 tablespoons parsley, finely chopped
1 teaspoon dried dill weed
1/4 teaspoon black pepper

- Rinse and pick over the beans, removing shriveled ones. Place beans in a 3-quart pan and pour boiling water over.
- Cover pan, bring to a boil; boil 2 minutes. Let stand for 1 hour.
- Simmer beans for 1 to 1 1/2 hours or until tender.
- Stir in salt after beans are tender.
- Beans can be done the day before. Cool and refrigerate. Heat beans before completing the recipe.
- Heat a small skillet; add olive oil, then carrots.
- Cook a few minutes; add celery and garlic.
- Cook 3 or 4 minutes more; stir into hot beans.
- Stir in parsley, dill and pepper. This classic dish is usually served at room temperature. Canned beans can be substituted. Drain 2 cans (15-ounces each) cannellini beans. Heat beans before mixing with the cooked vegetables.

Red and Yellow Tomato Salad

Serves 4

A beautiful but very simple salad. Use any fresh herb or substitute minced parsley or chives.

8 lettuce leaves, washed and dried
2 ripe red tomatoes (about 1/2 pound)
2 ripe yellow tomatoes (about 1/2 pound)
1 teaspoon red wine vinegar
1/4 teaspoon each salt and pepper
2 tablespoons olive oil
2 tablespoons chopped fresh basil or mint

- Place lettuce on salad plates or arrange on a platter.
- Slice tomatoes thinly and arrange in alternate colors on lettuce. Can be done to here hours in advance. Cover and chill.
- Stir salt and pepper into vinegar; stir in oil and herbs.
- Spoon dressing over tomatoes just before serving.

Jalapeño Corn Muffins

12 muffins

Toasting the cornmeal first really brings out the flavor. Adding corn and peppers makes marvelous muffins.

1 cup yellow cornmeal
1 cup unbleached white flour
1 1/2 teaspoons baking powder
1/2 teaspoon baking soda
1/2 teaspoon salt
1 cup whole kernel corn (frozen or canned)
1 jalapeño pepper, seeds removed, finely diced
1 egg
3/4 cup buttermilk
1/4 cup vegetable oil

- Heat oven to 350°. Spread the cornmeal on a baking sheet.
- Place cornmeal in the heated oven for 10 minutes to toast. Scrape toasted cornmeal into a bowl.
- Change oven temperature to 400°. Oil 12 muffin tins.
- Add to cornmeal the flour, baking powder, soda and salt.
- In a bowl, beat the egg lightly; add buttermilk and oil.
- Have corn at room temperature. If using canned corn, drain it. If frozen, thaw kernels. Mix with seeded, diced pepper.
- Combine the wet ingredients with the dry, stirring as little as possible to combine, adding corn and peppers after 15 strokes.
- Fill 12 muffin tins (2 1/2 inch) about two-thirds full.
- Bake 20 to 25 minutes until lightly browned on top.
- Remove muffins to a rack to cool, or put in a napkin-lined basket to serve at once.

Pineapple Ice Box Dessert

Serves 8

This was my mother's favorite party dessert. It is incredibly delicious and simple to make.

8 ounces plain sugar wafers, divided
1/3 cup butter
1/2 cup powdered sugar
1/4 cup pasteurized "egg beaters"
1 can (20 oz.) crushed pineapple, drained
8 ounces whipped topping or whipped cream

- Lightly butter a 6 x 10-inch glass or ceramic dish.
- Set pineapple to drain for at least one hour. Pineapple must be very well drained.
- Divide wafers in half; put one half at a time into a plastic or brown bag and crush with a rolling pin into fine crumbs.
- Spread crumbs in the buttered dish for the bottom layer.
- Cream butter and powdered sugar together, slowly beat in the "egg beaters." Spread gently on crumbs as the next layer.
- Spread the well-drained pineapple evenly as the next layer.
- Drop spoonfuls of whipped topping or whipped cream on pineapple, and smooth over gently for an even layer.
- Crush remaining sugar wafers into crumbs for the top layer.
- Cover pan; set in refrigerator to chill 10 hours or overnight.
- Cut in squares; serve on individual dessert plates.

Chicken Paprika on Noodles
Green Beans Lyonnaise
Romaine Salad with Herb Croutons
Strawberry Shortcakes

Chicken Paprika

Serves 4

Chefs usually make this recipe with Hungarian rose paprika, but any fresh paprika will do. Paprika will stay fresh if refrigerated.

1 frying chicken (about 3 pounds) cut into 8 or 9 pieces
2 tablespoons vegetable oil
1/2 cup chopped onion
1 clove garlic, minced
1 teaspoon salt
1 tablespoon paprika
1 can (6 oz.) tomato paste
1 cup water or chicken broth
2 tablespoons flour
1/4 cup cold water
3/4 cup sour cream, at room temperature

- Rinse chicken pieces and dry on paper towels.
- Heat a dutch oven or heavy pan; add the oil and onion.
- Cook a few minutes; add garlic and salt; cook 2 minutes.
- Stir in the paprika, tomato paste, water or chicken broth. Cook a few minutes to blend.
- Add the chicken; cover and cook over low heat until chicken is tender, about 45 to 50 minutes, turning once.
- Remove chicken to a serving bowl and keep warm.
- There should be about 1 to 1 1/2 cups broth in pan.
- Stir the flour into 1/4 cup cold water, whisk into the hot broth and whisk constantly until sauce is thickened and bubbly.
- Add sour cream last, and heat just a minute. Don't boil.
- Pour the hot sauce over chicken pieces or pass it separately.

Preparing the Noodles:

Pasta varies in the amount of time it takes to get tender. Keep tasting to prevent overcooking.

12 ounces broad noodles
3 quarts water
1 teaspoon salt

- Bring water to a boil, add noodles and salt. Boil, uncovered, until tender but firm. Taste one from time to time to test doneness.

Helpful Hint

Pasta can be cooked hours or even days ahead. Immediately after pasta is cooked to your taste and drained, put it back into the pan with 1 tablespoon of olive oil. Toss in the oil so strands do not stick together, cool, and keep covered in refrigerator.

Green Beans Lyonnaise
Serves 4

1 package (10 oz.) frozen green beans
or 3/4 pound fresh green beans, trimmed
1 small onion, thinly sliced
2 tablespoons butter or margarine
1/2 teaspoon salt
Dash each of pepper and nutmeg

- Drop frozen beans into boiling water and cook just long enough to be tender but crisp.
- If fresh beans are used, bring 2 quarts of water to a boil, add beans and cook 6 to 7 minutes, until tender but crisp.
- In a skillet, lightly fry the onion in butter until soft.
- Drain beans, toss with onions, salt, pepper and nutmeg.

Romaine Salad

Serves 4

A crisp green salad with a tangy dressing refreshes the palate and is wonderfully healthy. Try this with red-tipped lettuce, too.

3/4 pound romaine lettuce
3 tablespoons Herb Dressing
1 cup herb croutons

- Wash romaine; dry leaves on a towel. Tear or slice lettuce into bite size pieces. Keep covered.
- Have dressing and croutons prepared ahead.
- Just before serving, toss lettuce in a big bowl with the dressing until leaves are well coated.
- Add croutons and toss.

Herb Croutons

These are best made with slightly stale bread.

2 thick slices whole wheat or French bread
2 teaspoons olive oil
1/2 teaspoon dried basil
1/2 teaspoon dried oregano

- Cut bread into half-inch cubes. Put on baking sheet.
- Heat oven to 350°. Bake cubes 10 to 12 minutes.
- Mix oil with herbs in a bowl, add croutons and toss well.
- Store in a tightly covered glass jar in refrigerator.

Helpful Hint

Croutons keep for several days. In the interests of economy, make a batch of croutons while something else is baking in the oven, like a loaf of bread or a casserole.

Strawberry Shortcakes

Serves 4

Combine a sweet tender biscuit with berries in season for an unbeatable summer dessert.

1 cup flour
2 tablespoons sugar
1 1/2 teaspoons baking powder
1/4 teaspoon salt
3 tablespoons cold butter or margarine
1/4 cup milk

• Heat oven to 425°. Lightly oil a baking sheet.

• Sift flour, sugar, baking powder and salt into a bowl

• Cut in the butter or margarine with a pastry blender or two knives until mixture resembles coarse crumbs.

• Stir in enough milk to make a soft dough, turn out on a lightly floured surface, and knead together 10 times.

• Pat into a square and cut into 4 pieces. Place on pan.

• Bake in the hot oven for 20 minutes, until lightly browned on top. Keep warm until serving time.

Assembling the shortcakes:

1 pint fresh berries, rinsed
1 to 3 tablespoons sugar
Whipped cream or vanilla ice cream

• Hull berries and cut in halves. Quarter the larger berries.

• Add sugar to berries gradually, tasting for sweetness.

• Split each biscuit in half horizontally, put the bottom half on a dessert plate, and top with a spoonful of berries.

• Place other half of biscuit on top and spoon on berries.

• If desired, add a dollop of whipped cream or put a scoop of vanilla ice cream on the plate.

Oven-Crisp Fish Nuggets
Baked Stuffed Potatoes
Broccoli Italian Style
Garden Salad with Chutney Dressing
Nesselrode Pie with Chocolate Curls

Oven-Crisp Fish Nuggets

Serves 4

Any white fish fillet can be used for these crunchy treats. Catfish, a firm white fish with excellent flavor, is a thrifty choice.

1 pound fresh fish nuggets
1 small can (5 oz.) evaporated milk
3/4 cup crushed cornflakes or bread crumbs
2 tablespoons chopped almonds, toasted
3/4 teaspoon celery salt
1/4 teaspoon paprika
nonstick cooking spray
1 lemon, cut into 8 wedges, for garnish

- Lightly oil a large baking sheet. Heat oven to 375°.
- Pat fish nuggets dry on a paper towel.
- Pour evaporated milk into a shallow bowl.
- Mix corn flakes, almonds and seasonings in a shallow bowl.
- Dip nuggets into the milk, then into cornflake mixture.
- Place nuggets on baking sheet. Recipe can be done to here one hour ahead. If done ahead, cover and chill fish.
- Spray fish lightly with nonstick cooking spray.
- Bake 25 minutes, until brown and crisp. If chunks are large, turn pieces once during baking to brown evenly.
- Serve fish with wedges of lemon.

Baked Stuffed Potatoes

Serves 4

These are also called twice-baked potatoes, and everyone loves them. The stuffing can be varied by adding grated cheese or a few chopped, cooked mushrooms.

4 medium baking potatoes (1 1/2 pounds)
1/3 cup milk
1 tablespoon butter or margarine
2 green onions, with tops
1/2 teaspoon salt
Paprika

- Heat oven to 450°. Wash and dry potatoes.

- Bake potatoes about 1 hour until soft. Cool a few minutes.

- Cut a thin slice horizontally off top of potato.

- Scoop out centers, being careful not to break the skin.

- Mash potato, beating in the milk and butter, until fluffy.

- Stir in the chopped green onions and salt.

- Spoon mashed potato into the shells, rounding tops.

- Place potatoes in a baking dish.

- Sprinkle tops with paprika.

- These can be done to here several hours ahead.

- Bake the stuffed potatoes at 375° for 20 minutes.

Broccoli Italian Style

Serves 4

Don't discard stems of broccoli; they have a delicious flavor all their own. Always undercook broccoli to retain crispness.

3/4 to 1 pound broccoli
1 tablespoon olive oil
2 cloves garlic, crushed, sliced thinly
Salt and pepper

- Choose a dark green head of broccoli with tight buds.
- Submerge the head in cool water to rinse thoroughly.
- Trim off the ends of stalks. Cut off the florets.
- Peel the stems and cut into thin matchsticks 2 inches long.
- Place a large steamer basket over boiling water.
- Steam broccoli about 5 minutes, until tender but firm.
- Drain broccoli; keep warm.
- Heat a nonstick skillet; add oil and garlic.
- Stir-fry half a minute, then add broccoli to pan and mix well.
- Sprinkle with salt and pepper and serve hot.

Garden Salad with Chutney Dressing

Serves 4

A marvelous assortment of lettuces are in our markets: Boston, Bibb, curly endive, romaine, red tipped and green leaf. Enjoy any combination of fresh crisp greens.

4 cups lettuce, torn up
1 tomato, diced
1 small cucumber, sliced
4 radishes, sliced
2 green onions, sliced

- Have lettuce leaves well washed and dried.
- Wrap in a towel and chill until serving time.
- Wash and dice vegetables; keep chilled.
- Toss lettuce and vegetables with dressing just before serving.

Chutney Dressing

2 tablespoons chutney (page 137)
2 tablespoons lemon juice or vinegar
1/2 teaspoon salt
3 tablespoons vegetable oil

- Measure ingredients into a blender. Blend until mixed.
- Just before serving, shake up dressing and toss with salad.

Nesselrode Pie with Chocolate Curls

An elegant dessert , so easy to make the day before. The chocolate curls as a finishing touch are easy, too.

1 prepared (6 oz.) chocolate pie crust
1 tablespoon unflavored gelatin
1/4 cup cold water
2 eggs, separated
a pinch of salt
2 cups whole milk or half-and-half
1/2 cup sugar, divided
1 teaspoon rum flavoring
a small chocolate bar for curls

- Combine the gelatin and cold water in a small bowl.

- Beat egg yolks with 1/4 cup sugar; add pinch of salt.

- Bring milk to a boil in the top of a double boiler.

- Add a little hot milk to eggs, beat, then add rest of the milk.

- Put pan over hot water and cook custard 10 to 15 minutes, stirring constantly, until smooth and thickened. Add the softened gelatin and whisk to completely dissolve.

- Pour into a cold bowl and chill in refrigerator for 1 hour. Mixture will be quite thick.

- Beat the egg whites until stiff, beating in 1/4 cup sugar and the rum flavoring.

- Gently fold the beaten whites into the cooled custard.

- Pour into the chocolate pie shell; chill until firm.This can be done a day ahead.

- Use a vegetable peeler to shave thin curls of chocolate onto the top of the pie. Have chocolate at room temperature.

> **Stuffed Green Peppers**
> **Country Corn Pudding**
> **Molded Cucumber Salad**
> **Onion Rolls**
> **Poached Pears with Chocolate Sauce**

Stuffed Green Peppers

Serves 4

Flavorful and nutritious, sweet bell peppers serve very well as shells for an herb-accented rice filling.

2 large sweet green peppers
2 cups cooked rice
2 tablespoons olive oil
1 large onion, chopped small
1/2 teaspoon salt
1 can (16 oz.) tomatoes, divided
1/2 teaspoon dried basil
1/2 teaspoon dried oregano
1 teaspoon honey

- Slice peppers in half lengthwise and remove seeds.
- Drop peppers into boiling water and cook 5 minutes.
- Turn peppers upside down to drain.
- Heat a nonstick skillet and add oil. Add onion.
- Add salt and lightly fry the onion until soft.
- Mix half the tomatoes with the herbs, the cooked rice and the onions. Spoon mixture into the shells.
- Puree remaining tomatoes with the honey in a blender.
- Spoon pureed tomatoes over peppers.
- Place stuffed peppers in a buttered shallow baking dish.
- Bake at 375° for 30 minutes.

Country Corn Pudding
Serves 4

A delectable dish with a custard-like texture and a mellow flavor.

8 saltine crackers, crushed into crumbs
2 eggs, lightly beaten
1/4 cup milk
1 can (15 oz.) cream-style corn
1 tablespoon melted butter or margarine
1/2 teaspoon salt
1/4 teaspoon paprika

* Spray a 1-quart baking dish with nonstick cooking spray.

* Heat oven to 350°.

* In a mixing bowl, combine the lightly beaten eggs with the milk; stir in the creamed corn, butter and salt.

* Pour into prepared baking dish; top with the crushed cracker crumbs. Sprinkle top with paprika.

* Place baking dish in a pan of hot water. Put in oven.

* Bake until set, or a knife inserted in center comes out clean, about 50 minutes.

* Remove from oven; serve at once.

Helpful Hint

Don't throw stale crackers away; they can be refreshed. Put them on a baking pan in a single layer and put into a moderate oven (350°) for 4 to 6 minutes. Check to make sure they do not scorch. Or use a microwave oven, using high power for just a minute. Microwave ovens vary so check to get the time right for your own oven.

Molded Cucumber Salad

Serves 6

Cool, green, and shimmering, a refreshing salad you can make the day before the dinner.

1 small package lime gelatin dessert
3/4 cup hot water
2 tablespoons lemon juice
1 teaspoon onion juice
1 medium-size cucumber, peeled
1/2 cup light sour cream
1/2 cup light mayonnaise

- Dissolve the gelatin dessert in the hot water, stirring.

- Add the lemon juice and onion juice. Cool.

- Shred cucumber on coarse side of a grater. There should be about 1 cup. Place in strainer to remove excess liquid.

- Fold the cucumber into the gelatin; add sour cream and mayonnaise.

- Pour into 8 x 8-inch dish, or individual molds. Chill until set.

- To serve, cut into squares and place on lettuce leaves.

Helpful Hint

To obtain onion juice, cut an onion in half and scrape across the onion with the flat side of a knife.

Onion Rolls

Makes 16 rolls

A crusty outside, the goodness of whole wheat and onion flavors inside, these are a treat you will serve with pride.

2 teaspoons quick-acting yeast
1 cup warm water, divided
1 teaspoon sugar
2 tablespoons oil, divided
1 cup unbleached white flour
2 to 2 1/2 cups whole wheat flour
1 teaspoon salt, divided
1 large onion, finely diced

- Put yeast, sugar and 1/4 cup of the warm water in a bowl. Let stand 5 minutes until foamy.
- Add remaining 3/4 cup water, 1 tablespoon of the oil, 3 cups of the flour and 1/2 teaspoon of the salt.
- Stir together, working with your hand as it gets stiff.
- Sprinkle some of the remaining flour on a work surface and turn out dough, kneading about 5 minutes until dough is smooth and elastic, and working in more flour as needed.
- Lightly oil a bowl; put dough in bowl and turn around to coat.
- Cover with a towel and keep in a warm place about 1 hour, until dough has risen to double in size.
- While dough is rising, heat a skillet; add 1 tablespoon oil.
- Add the onions and 1/2 teaspoon salt and cook over medium heat for 30 minutes, until onions are soft and beginning to brown. Set aside.
- When the dough has risen, punch down and work in the fried onions. Some will remain outside, which is desirable.
- Spray a baking sheet with nonstick cooking spray.
- Divide dough into 16 balls. Place balls on baking sheet.
- Let rise 30 minutes. Heat oven to 400°.
- Bake rolls for 20 minutes. Remove from pan to rack to cool.

Poached Pears with Chocolate Sauce

Serves 6

This elegant dessert is ever so simple to make. You may see something like it on menus of sophisticated restaurants as "Pears Helene." Use large, firm pears.

To poach pears:

3 fresh, firm Bosc or Anjou pears
1 cup water
1/2 cup sugar
1 teaspoon vanilla extract

• Peel pears, cut in half lengthwise and remove cores and seeds.

• Bring water and sugar to a boil in a wide shallow pan (I use a Visionware skillet); add pear halves.

• Cover, reduce heat to low; simmer for 20 to 30 minutes. Cook only until pears are tender when pierced with the tip of a knife; don't overcook. Remove from heat.

• Add vanilla to syrup in the pan and let pears cool in the syrup.

For Chocolate Sauce:

1/2 cup sugar
1/4 cup unsweetened cocoa powder
1/4 cup light corn syrup
1/4 cup water
1 teaspoon butter or margarine
1 teaspoon vanilla extract

• Sift sugar and cocoa into a small pan. Add water and corn syrup. Bring to a boil over medium heat, stirring.

• Boil 3 minutes, stirring occasionally. Remove from heat and stir in butter or margarine and vanilla. Serve warm. Makes about 1 1/2 cups.

• Chocolate sauce can be prepared several days or even weeks ahead. Store in the refrigerator in a pint canning jar, covered. The sauce gets very thick when cold. Before serving, heat opened jar in a small pan of hot water or in a microwave oven so it is warm and pours easily.

To serve:

1 pint vanilla ice cream or frozen yogurt

- Transfer one pear half, cut side up, to each dessert dish.
- Top pear with a scoop of ice cream or frozen yogurt.
- Drizzle warm chocolate sauce over each serving. Serve immediately.

> **Cantonese Beef and Vegetables**
> **Blueberry Muffins**
> **Apple Upside-down Tart**
> **Vanilla Sauce**

Cantonese Beef and Vegetables

Serves 4

Any variety of shredded vegetables can be used. Have 5 cups of vegetables in all. Shop with an eye for contrasting colors in vegetables. Meat is easier to slice thinly if frozen.

1 cup thinly sliced onions
1 cup carrots, cut lengthwise in thin matchsticks
1/2 cup celery, thinly sliced on the diagonal
1 cup broccoli florets or 1 cup green string
beans, sliced thinly on the diagonal
1 cup fresh bean sprouts or sliced cauliflower
1 can (8 oz.) sliced water chestnuts, drained
5 green onions, with tops, in 1/4 inch slices
1/2 pound beef sirloin, thinly sliced
1 tablespoon cornstarch
3 tablespoons soy sauce
2 teaspoons Worcestershire sauce
1 teaspoon salt
1/2 teaspoon sugar
1/2 cup vegetable broth, from cooking vegetables
4 tablespoons vegetable or peanut oil, divided
1 cup long grain or converted rice,
    to cook separately as accompaniment.

- Bring 1 cup water to a boil in a 2-quart saucepan. Drop in onions, carrots, celery, broccoli or cauliflower or green beans.
- Bring water to a boil again and parboil vegetables 1 minute only. Drain, saving water to use as vegetable broth.
- Mix cornstarch, soy, Worcestershire, salt and sugar in a bowl.
- Slice beef very thinly; stir meat into soy mixture.
- Meat and vegetables can be prepared to here in advance. Arrange the vegetables in a colorful circle on a large platter; have the sliced and marinated beef in a separate bowl. Invite your guests to the kitchen to see the last minute stir-fry.
- Cook 1 cup long grain rice and keep warm to serve with the beef and vegetables.

- Heat a large skillet or wok. Have a large serving bowl ready.
- Add half the oil to pan, stir in vegetables, sauté for 2 minutes, and remove to the serving dish. Do not overcook vegetables.
- Heat pan again, add remaining 2 tablespoons oil and stir fry the beef for just 1 minute. Beef should be rare.
- Return the vegetables to the pan with the warm vegetable broth. Bring all to a boil. Mix well and serve hot over the cooked rice.

Blueberry Muffins

Makes 12 muffins

These muffins make any meal a memorable occasion and it's easy to stir up a batch. When blueberries are in season and a bargain price, freeze some for winter treats.

1 cup blueberries. gently rinsed
1 cup whole wheat flour
1 cup unbleached white flour
1/3 cup sugar
2 teaspoons baking powder
1/2 teaspoon baking soda
1/4 teaspoon salt
1 egg, slightly beaten
1/4 cup vegetable oil
3/4 cup sour milk or yogurt

- Oil 12 (2 1/2-inch) muffin tins or line with paper baking cups..
- Heat oven to 400°. Drain rinsed berries well.
- In a mixing bowl, combine the flour, sugar, baking powder, salt and baking soda and mix together well.
- In another bowl, combine the slightly beaten egg, oil and milk.
- Combine in as few strokes as possible the dry ingredients with the wet ingredients, adding blueberries after 15 strokes. Mix only enough to blend, so muffins will be light and fluffy.
- Divide batter evenly into the muffin cups. Bake 20 to 25 minutes, until they are lightly browned on top. Run a knife around edge of tins to loosen muffins and remove from pans at once. Serve hot.

Apple Upside-down Tart

Serves 5

This tart is brimming with old fashioned flavor, and is simplicity itself to make. It's also excellent made with ripe pears.

4 large apples, peeled, cored, sliced
1 tablespoon butter or margarine
2 tablespoons brown sugar
1/2 teaspoon cinnamon

Topping:

1 1/2 cups flour
1 1/2 teaspoons baking powder
2 tablespoons sugar
1/4 teaspoon salt
1/4 cup vegetable oil
1/4 cup milk
1 teaspoon vanilla extract

- Heat a large skillet, melt the butter, and add the sliced apples.
- Sprinkle with sugar and cinnamon. Cook over low heat about 15 minutes. Stir occasionally so apples cook evenly.
- In a bowl, stir topping ingredients together.
- Heat oven to 400°.
- Put apples in a 9-inch pie pan; spoon topping over apples.
- Bake 20 to 25 minutes, until top is lightly browned.
- Remove from oven. Run a knife around edge of pan to loosen.
- Invert onto a round platter or plate, handling hot pan carefully. Serve warm.
- This can be served with a scoop of ice cream or frozen yogurt on the side, or try a simple creamy sauce like Vanilla Sauce.

Vanilla Sauce

This is a less expensive version of the classic and rich Creme Anglaise of French cuisine.

1 tablespoon cornstarch
2 tablespoons sugar
2/3 cup half-and-half or milk
1 teaspoon vanilla extract

- Mix the sugar and cornstarch in a small saucepan. Whisk in the half-and-half or milk.

- Cook over moderate heat, whisking constantly, until sauce thickens and bubbles.

- Remove from heat; whisk in vanilla.

- Keep covered until serving time. Whisk just before serving.

Linguine with Fresh Asparagus
Tomato Aspic Salad
Zucchini Muffins
Fresh Peach Melba

Linguine with Fresh Asparagus

Serves 4

A springtime delight when fresh asparagus arrives in the market.

6 ounces (about 8 stalks) fresh asparagus
8 ounces linguine or thin spaghetti
1 jar (2 oz.) red pimientos
1 tablespoon olive oil
1 cup onion, chopped small
1/2 teaspoon salt
2 cloves garlic, smashed, sliced, peels removed
2 tablespoons Parmesan cheese

- Wash asparagus; snap off tough ends. Peel lower part of stems. Cut stalks on the diagonal into 2-inch lengths.

- Drop asparagus into a pan of boiling water and boil for 2 minutes. Drain.

- Drain pimientos, cut into small strips and set aside.

- Bring 3 quarts salted water to a boil; add pasta. Cook pasta until tender but firm, 8 to 10 minutes, tasting to test doneness.

- Heat a skillet; add oil and swirl around to coat the bottom.

- Add the chopped onion and salt and cook 5 minutes, stirring.

- Add garlic, cook a minute, then add asparagus. Stir fry.

- After asparagus is hot, add pimientos to pan and mix well.

- Toss vegetables with drained pasta and Parmesan cheese.

Tomato Aspic Salad

Serves 6

Aspic is a cool, shimmering jelly with a piquant flavor, and came to us as part of our French culinary heritage

2 tablespoons (2 envelopes) plain gelatin
1/4 cup cold water
2 cups tomato juice
1 small onion, sliced
2 tablespoons vinegar
4 sprigs parsley
4 whole cloves
1 bay leaf
1 teaspoon sugar
1/2 teaspoon salt
1/2 cup finely diced celery or 1/2 cup sliced stuffed olives

- Stir gelatin in the cold water to soften; set aside.
- Bring to a boil the tomato juice, onion, vinegar, parsley, and seasonings. Reduce heat and simmer about 15 minutes.
- Strain; discard solids, pressing liquid through strainer.
- Return liquid to pan and stir in the gelatin; simmer a few minutes to completely dissolve. Cool.
- Stir in the chopped celery, or sliced stuffed olives.
- Pour into 6 individual molds or an 8 x 8-inch pan.
- Chill until firm. Unmold or cut into squares to serve on a bed of lettuce with mayonnaise.

Zucchini Muffins

Makes 12

Round, golden brown on the outside with flecks of green inside, these fragrant little muffins are a savory accompaniment.

1 egg, lightly beaten
1/4 cup oil
1 small zucchini (about 4 ounces)
2 teaspoons dried onion flakes
3/4 cup buttermilk
2 tablespoons sugar
2 cups unbleached white flour
2 teaspoons baking powder
1/2 teaspoon baking soda
1/2 teaspoon salt

- Spray well 12 (2 1/2-inch) muffin tins with nonstick cooking spray, or line tins with paper baking cups.

- Heat oven to 400°.

- Trim ends from zucchini; wash, and shred on the coarse side of a grater. You will have about 1 cup of shredded zucchini.

- Combine in a mixing bowl the lightly beaten egg, oil, zucchini, dried onion flakes and the buttermilk.

- Measure the dry ingredients into a clean bowl and stir well.

- Add the dry ingredients to the wet ingredeints and stir only until wet and dry are mixed.

- Spoon batter into the prepared muffin tins.

- Bake about 25 minutes, until tops are golden brown.

- Remove from oven; run a knife around edge of each muffin to loosen from tin and immediately remove from pan.

Chicken Pie with Cornbread Topping
Sweet Potatoes with Pecans
Grapefruit Red Pepper Salad
Orange Soy Dressing
Banana Nut Cake with Cream Cheese Icing

Chicken Pie with Cornbread Topping

Serves 4 to 6

This old fashioned favorite takes time, but the work can be done one or two days in advance; add topping just before baking.

Preparing the chicken:

> 2 chicken breasts, split (about 1 pound)
> 1 onion, cut in quarters
> 1 medium-size carrot, cut in chunks
> 1 rib celery, cut up, with leaves
> 4 sprigs of parsley
> 1/2 teaspoon salt
> 1 quart water

- Combine chicken, vegetables and water in a 3 quart kettle; cover and simmer about 35 to 45 minutes, until chicken is tender when pierced with the tip of a knife. Cool in the broth.
- This can be done 2 days ahead; cool and refrigerate. Bring to room temperature before proceeding.
- Remove and discard skin and bones. Strain the broth and save, discarding vegetables. Measure broth for gravy.

Preparing pie vegetables:

> 1 onion, chopped
> 2 medium-size carrots, diced
> 1 cup celery, diced
> 2 cups water
> 1 cup frozen or canned peas, drained
> 1 cup fresh or frozen corn (optional)

- Place onions, carrots and celery in a 2-quart pan; add water, cover, bring to a boil and cook 10 minutes.
- Drain and save vegetable broth. Stir peas and corn in with the hot vegetables. Cool the broth to use in the gravy.

Preparing the gravy:

2 tablespoons butter or margarine
3 tablespoons unbleached white flour
2 cups chicken broth
1/2 teaspoon dried thyme
Salt and pepper to taste

- Measure broth left from cooking the chicken, and add enough of the vegetable broth to make 2 cups.
- Melt butter or margarine in a 2-quart pan, whisk in the flour, making a smooth paste, and gradually add the broth, whisking to keep it smooth.
- Cook over low heat until gravy thickens and bubbles. Taste gravy; add a little salt and pepper if needed.

Assembling the pie:

- Mix chicken, gravy, and vegetables in a wide 2-quart casserole that is 2 to 3 inches deep.
- Heat oven to 350°,
- Heat chicken, gravy and vegetables until bubbling hot.
- The chicken, vegetables and gravy can be assembled ahead. Cover and chill. Heat the chicken and gravy in the oven until hot before putting on the topping.

Cornbread Topping:

1 (7 1/2 oz.) package corn muffin mix
1/2 cup milk or vegetable broth

- Whisk muffin mix and liquid in a small bowl until blended.
- Drop by spoonfuls on top of hot chicken mixture, spreading evenly. Crust may be soggy unless the chicken gravy is hot when the cornbread batter is put on the pie.
- Return casserole to the hot oven for 15 minutes to bake the topping.

Sweet Potatoes with Pecans

Serves 4 to 6

A friend in Charleston, S.C. gave me this recipe from the Old South. Potatoes can also be baked, then mashed.

4 medium sweet potatoes (about 1 1 /4 pounds)
2 tablespoons butter or margarine
1/2 teaspoon salt
1/4 cup pecans, chopped coarsely
3 tablespoons brown sugar

- Bring 2 quarts of water to a boil.
- Peel sweet potatoes; cut in half. Drop in water and cook until tender, about 20 minutes. Lift out with a slotted spoon to drain.
- Place potatoes in a mixing bowl and mash, adding the butter or margarine and the salt.
- Lightly butter a 1-quart casserole; heap potatoes into dish.
- Sprinkle with the pecans and brown sugar.
- This can be done to here the day before. Cover and refrigerate. Bring to room temperature before baking.
- Heat oven to 350°.
- Bake potatoes 25 to 30 minutes.

Grapefruit Red Pepper Salad

Serves 4

A salad that adds a tangy crispness to the menu, contrasting nicely with a mellow main dish.

1/2 head romaine or iceberg lettuce
1 large grapefruit, peeled
1 sweet red pepper, thinly sliced
2 tablespoons purple onion, chopped

- Wash lettuce, cut to bite size and arrange on salad plates.
- Cut grapefruit in half, slice, arrange on lettuce.
- Top with rings of thinly sliced red pepper; sprinkle with finely chopped purple onion.
- Serve with Orange Soy Dressing.

Orange Soy Dressing

This perky dressing is adapted from Miyoko Nishimoto's book, "The Now and Zen Epicure."

2 tablespoons orange or grapefruit juice
1 tablespoon soy sauce
1 tablespoon white vinegar
1/4 cup vegetable oil

- Whisk ingredients together until thickened. Whisk just before spooning over the salads.

Banana Nut Cake

Makes 8 pieces

This delicious cake is a great way to use overripe bananas, and a food processor will make the batter quickly.

2 ripe bananas
1 egg
1/4 cup vegetable oil
2/3 cup sugar
1 1/2 cups unbleached white flour
1 teaspoon baking powder
1/2 teaspoon baking soda
1/3 cup sour milk
1 teaspoon vanilla extract
1/2 cup walnuts, toasted

- Heat oven to 350°. Place walnuts on a baking sheet; put in oven for 5 to 6 minutes. Cool.
- Spray 6 x 10-inch baking pan with nonstick cooking spray.
- In a food processor, mash bananas; add egg, oil and sugar.
- Add sour milk, vanilla and process. Mix in flour, baking powder and soda. When well blended, stir in walnuts by hand.
- Pour into prepared pan and bake for 40 to 45 minutes.
- Cool cake before frosting. Cut in squares to serve.

Cream Cheese Icing

Calorie counters can make this with "lite" cream cheese.

1 (3-oz.) package cream cheese
1 tablespoon butter or margarine
1 cup powdered sugar
2 teaspoons grated orange rind
1 teaspoon vanilla extract

- Mash the cream cheese with the butter or margarine.
- Slowly mash in the sugar, orange rind and vanilla.
- Mixture should be spreadable; if not, add a few drops of water.
- Spread evenly over top of cooled cake.

Baked Cheese Enchiladas
Mexican Rice
Refried Beans
Pink Onion Rings
Strawberry Cream Pie

Baked Cheese Enchiladas

Serves 4

Savor the flavors of this authentic Mexican recipe.The sauce is easy, cheap and better than canned. Most of the oil set out for frying will be left over and can be used later for other frying.

Enchilada Sauce:

> 2 tablespoons vegetable oil
> 2/3 cup onion, chopped small
> 1/2 teaspoon salt
> 2 tablespoons chili powder
> 1 teaspoon cumin powder
> 1/2 teaspoon garlic powder
> 1/4 cup flour
> 4 cups water

- Heat a 2-quart saucepan and swirl oil around to coat pan.
- Add onion and salt; cook 5 minutes until onion is soft.
- Stir in chili powder, cumin and garlic powder.
- Sprinkle with the flour; stir well. Stir in the water.
- Simmer over low heat for 25 to 30 minutes, whisking from time to time as it cooks down. If sauce is lumpy, whiz in blender.
- Makes about 3 cups.This can be made 2 or 3 days ahead.

To assemble:

1 package (6 oz.) corn tortillas (10 tortillas)
1/2 cup oil for frying tortillas
Enchilada Sauce (see recipe)
8 ounces Monterey Jack cheese, shredded
3/4 cup white onion, diced

- Have tortillas at room temperature. Lightly spray a 9 x 13-inch shallow baking pan. Have a plate ready for dipped tortillas.
- Have enchilada sauce ready in a wide, shallow bowl.
- Have shredded cheese and onion set out in bowls next to plate of tortillas and the baking pan.
- Heat the oil in a 10-inch heavy skillet
- Using tongs, hold corn tortilla in hot oil for a few seconds, turning over to soften both sides. Lift tortilla from oil, shaking any excess oil into the pan. At once, dip tortilla into the bowl of sauce and lay it on a plate. Continue dipping tortillas into hot oil and then into sauce until all 10 are done.
- Working quickly with the warm tortillas, put about 2 tablespoons of the shredded cheese down center of each tortilla and sprinkle with about 1 tablespoon of onion.
- Fold sides over and place seam side down in the baking dish.
- Repeat this procedure until all tortillas have been filled and placed side by side in the baking pan.
- Pour remaining sauce on top of enchiladas. Sprinkle leftover cheese on top. These can be done to here 30 minutes before baking. Keep covered with foil and a towel.
- Heat oven to 350°, uncover dish, and bake 15 to 20 minutes until cheese is melted and sauce bubbling.
- Arrange the following on a platter to serve as accompaniment:
    Pink Onion Rings (see recipe)
    Shredded lettuce
    Sliced avocado (optional)

Mexican Rice

Serves 4

When I order the "Mexican Plate" at my favorite cafe in Mazatlan, it has a scoop of rice similar to this on it.

1 carrot, diced very small (about 1/2 cup)
1 cup white long grain rice
2 1/2 cups vegetable broth
1 teaspoon vegetable oil
1/2 teaspoon salt
1/4 teaspoon paprika

- Bring broth to a boil and drop in diced carrot.
- Cook 3 minutes; add rice, oil and salt. Cover pan. Bring to a boil, reduce heat to low; stir once or twice.
- Cook rice 10 to 12 minutes, until rice is tender and the liquid is absorbed. Fluff with a fork before serving with a dash of paprika.

Refried Beans

Serves 4

These delicious beans are poorly named, as they are not really fried at all. The liquid is slowly cooked down until beans are dry.

1 can (15-oz.) pinto or black beans
1/4 cup onion, diced very fine
2 teaspoons vegetable oil

• Drain beans, discarding 2 tablespoons of the liquid, and reserving the remaining liquid.

• Heat a small skillet; add oil and onion and cook over low heat until onion is soft, about 5 minutes.

• Add beans and remaining liquid. Mash with a potato masher until beans are mostly pureed but retain some chunky bits. Cook slowly about 30 minutes to dry out the beans, stirring often to bring browned bits up from the bottom. These can be made one hour ahead to serve at room temperature.

• Serve a scoop of beans on each plate.

Pink Onion Rings

Sharp-tasting onions become mild for this attractive garnish.

2 cups boiling water
1/2 of a large purple onion, cut horizontally
1/4 cup cold water
1/4 cup white vinegar
1/2 teaspoon salt

- Bring water to a boil.
- Cut 5 or 6 very thin round slices from a fat purple onion; remove onion peel after slicing.
- Separate onions into rings; place in a large bowl.
- Pour boiling water over onion rings; let stand 2 minutes, stir.
- Mix the cold water, vinegar and salt in another bowl.
- Drain onion rings, place in vinegar mix and let stand for 30 minutes. Drain; cover and chill until serving time.
- Arrange rings on shredded lettuce on dinner plates or serving platter, adding slices of avocado if desired.

Helpful Hint

To peel an avocado, work a knife lengthwise around the seed, cutting full circle. Twist the sides of the avocado to pull apart into halves. Remove pit Cut the flesh down from tip to stem in several pieces and peel off the skin. This will give you perfect slices of velvety green ripe avocado. Do not peel until just before serving, as it will darken on standing unless covered with lemon juice.

Strawberry Cream Pie

Serves 6

Strawberries are very good in Mexico and served many ways. This is an easy do-ahead dessert to serve with a Mexican meal.

One crumb crust (page 137) or a chocolate ready-made pie crust
Cream Pie Filling:

1 1/2 cups milk
1/2 cup sugar
3 tablespoons unbleached white flour
1/4 teaspoon salt
2 eggs, beaten
1 tablespoon butter or margarine
1 teaspoon vanilla extract

* Scald 1 cup of the milk in the top of a double boiler.

* Mix the sugar, flour and salt in a small bowl, stir the remaining 1/2 cup milk into the dry ingredients, and mix to a smooth paste.

* Pour this into the hot milk; cook and stir until it is thick.

* Beat eggs, Stir a little of the hot mixture slowly into the eggs, then add the egg mixture to sauce in the pan.

* Cook 5 minutes longer, stirring to keep smooth.

* Remove from heat; stir in butter and vanilla. Cool.

* When filling is cool, pour into the crumb shell. Chill.

Strawberry Topping:

1 pint strawberries
2 tablespoons sugar, if needed

* Rinse berries, slice, and add sugar to taste. Chill.

* Just before serving pie, spoon berries evenly over top.

Fish Fillets Vera Cruz
Rice and Onion Pilaf
Romaine Salad with Avocado Dressing
Skillet Corn Bread
Lemon Yogurt Cake

Fish Fillets Vera Cruz

Serves 4

The vibrant flavors and colors of Spain tempt the tastebuds in this exciting entree.

4 fish fillets, about 1 pound
2 tablespoons vegetable oil, divided
1 medium onion, chopped (1 cup)
1 green pepper, diced (1 cup)
1 rib celery, diced (1/2 cup)
1/2 teaspoon salt
1 can (16-oz.) tomatoes, chopped
2 tablespoons minced cilantro or parsley

- Heat a large skillet and swirl 1 tablespoon oil around to coat bottom. Lay fillets in pan and lightly brown one side. Turn over and cook just 1 minute. Transfer fillets to a shallow baking dish.

- Heat skillet, add remaining oil and sauté onion, pepper and celery. Sprinkle with salt. Cook over low heat 10 minutes.

- Add tomatoes and let bubble up.

- Spoon vegetables gently over fish.

- Heat oven to 375°.

- Bake fish for 15 to 20 minutes.

- Sprinkle with minced cilantro or parsley.

Rice and Onion Pilaf

Serves 4 to 6

A make-ahead way to serve rice. Brown rice can be used; just cook the pilaf longer until the rice is tender.

1 tablespoon vegetable oil
1 medium-size onion, chopped small
1/2 teaspoon salt
1 cup long grain white rice
2 1/4 cups water or vegetable broth

- Heat a 2-quart pan, add oil and onion, stir, add salt.
- Shake pan and cook about 5 minutes until onion is soft.
- Add rice, stir, and cook 2 minutes more.
- Add water or broth, bring to a boil, reduce heat to low; cover pan, and cook rice until tender, 12 to 14 minutes.
- This can be prepared a day ahead. Cover and refrigerate.
- If prepared in advance, reheat rice in the oven in a covered dish. Add a little vegetable broth if rice seems dry.

Romaine Salad with Avocado Dressing

Serves 4

A friend in Martha's Vineyard made this for me and kindly gave me the recipe.

3/4 pound head of romaine lettuce

- Wash romaine well, dry leaves on a towel, and tear into bite-size pieces.
- Keep refrigerated in the towel until serving time.
- Just before serving, toss the romaine in a glass or wooden bowl with Avocado Dressing.

Avocado Dressing

1 ripe avocado
1 small clove garlic, minced fine
2 tablespoons olive oil
Juice of 1 lemon (about 2 tablespoons)
1/2 teaspoon salt
1/4 teaspoon ground cumin

- Have everything ready to make this at the last minute.
- Peel avocado; discard skin and pit. Put into a salad bowl and mash with a fork, adding garlic, oil, lemon juice, salt and cumin.
- When creamy and smooth, add the washed and dried romaine to the salad bowl. Mix lettuce well with the avocado.

Skillet Corn Bread

Makes 8 wedges

This is adapted from a recipe in "The Vegetarian Epicure" by Anna Thomas. An old black, cast iron skillet makes a great crusty bread, but a square baking pan can also be used.

1 cup unbleached white flour
1 cup yellow corn meal (preferably stone ground)
1/4 cup sugar
5 teaspoons baking powder
1/4 teaspoon salt
1 egg
1 cup milk
2 tablespoons oil, divided

- Heat oven to 375°. Put a 10-inch black cast iron skillet in the hot oven for 5 minutes; lift out carefully and put 1 tablespoon oil in the bottom of the hot pan and swirl it around to coat.
- Whisk the dry ingredients together in a mixing bowl. The 5 teaspoons of baking powder seems a lot but is not too much.
- In another bowl, beat egg lightly with milk; stir in remaining oil.
- Stir wet ingredients into dry and pour batter into the hot skillet.
- Put in oven at once and bake about 30 minutes; the top will be golden brown. Cut into 8 wedges to serve.
- Any leftover cornbread is delicious if split and toasted.

Lemon Yogurt Cake

Makes 16 slices

A light and lovely ending to a meal and just as good the next day. An electric mixer helps make it quickly.

**2 large eggs
1 3/4 cup sugar
1/2 cup vegetable oil
1 cup low-fat vanilla yogurt
2 teaspoons minced lemon rind
1 teaspoon pure lemon extract
3 cups unbleached white flour
1 1/2 teaspoons baking powder
1 teaspoon baking soda**

- Heat oven to 350° Lightly oil a bundt pan.
- In a mixing bowl, beat eggs and sugar together.
- Beat in oil, yogurt, lemon rind and extract.
- Measure into another bowl the flour, baking powder and soda.
- Whisk the dry ingredients together.
- Add flour mixture to yogurt mixture. Beat to mix well.
- Pour batter into the lightly oiled pan.
- Bake 40 to 45 minutes, or until golden, and the top of cake springs back when lightly pressed.
- Cool cake in pan for 5 minutes; invert onto a cake plate; cool.
- When cool, drizzle Lemon Glaze over top of cake.

Lemon Glaze

**1/2 cup powdered sugar, sifted
2 teaspoons minced lemon rind
1 teaspoon lemon juice
2 drops pure lemon extract**

- Stir ingredients together. Spoon over top of cooled cake.

Beef Ragout
Mashed Potatoes with Carrots
Summer Squash Medley
Lettuce with Thousand Island Dressing
White Chocolate Pie

Beef Ragout

Serves 4

Call it ragout or call it stew, the long, slow oven braising in this recipe brings out the flavor. You can substitute red wine for part of the water, if desired. A heavy pan is essential.

3/4 to 1 pound beef chuck, cut in 1-inch cubes
2 tablespoons vegetable oil
2 large onions, thinly sliced
1 teaspoon salt
1/4 teaspoon pepper
3 cloves garlic, smashed, chopped
2 cups water

- Heat a dutch oven over moderate heat; add half the oil.
- Add sliced onions, reduce heat, and cook slowly about 30 minutes, until onions are tender. Put onions into a bowl.
- Raise heat in pan, add remaining oil, add meat and stir.
- Sprinkle with salt and pepper.
- Cook until beef is browned; add garlic to pan, cook 1 minute.
- Return onions to pan, add water; cover the pan.
- Heat oven to 325°.
- Bake ragout about 2 hours until meat is very tender.
- This can be prepared one or two days in advance.

Mashed Potatoes with Carrots

Serves 4

Eyecatching orange draws attention to this combination of healthy vegetables. For an even more intriguing flavor, instead of carrots, try a rutabaga, cooked, mashed and mixed with the mashed potato. It's a real winner.

4 medium potatoes, peeled
2 large carrots, peeled (or 1 rutabaga)
2 cups water
1 teaspoon salt
1 to 2 tablespoons olive oil or butter

- Bring water to a boil. Cut potatoes into quarters.

- Slice carrots into 2-inch chunks. Add salt to water.

- Drop potatoes and carrots into boiling water; cook 30 minutes, or until tender when pierced with a fork.

- Note: If substituting a rutabaga or yellow turnip, peel, dice and cook it separately from the potato. It may take longer to cook.

- Drain potatoes and carrots, saving vegetable water for broth.

- Mash vigorously until fluffy, adding the olive oil or butter.

- If potatoes seem at all dry, add a spoonful or two of the vegetable cooking water.

- Taste and add a little salt and pepper, if needed.

- These can be prepared ahead. Cover, reheat before serving.

Summer Squash Medley

Serves 4

This vegetable combination looks quite elegant on the plate and tastes delectable.
Use small, young squash.

2 small green zucchini (about 1/2 pound)
2 small yellow squash (about 1/2 pound)
1 medium onion, sliced thinly
2 cloves garlic, minced
2 tablespoons olive oil
1/2 teaspoon salt
1/8 teaspoon pepper
1/4 teaspoon dried oregano, crumbled

- Wash and trim ends from squash, but do not peel. Cut into julienne sticks about 2 inches long and 1/4 inch wide.
- Heat a large skillet, swirl oil around bottom, add onions and garlic. Cook 2 minutes, then stir in squash.
- Cover and cook over moderate heat about 5 minutes, or until squash just begins to appear transparent. Don't overcook.
- Season with salt, pepper and oregano and serve at once.

Thousand Island Dressing

Serve this robust, chunky dressing on wedges of crisp lettuce.

1/4 cup light mayonnaise
1/4 cup chili sauce
2 tablespoons chopped green pepper
1 teaspoon finely minced onion
1 hard cooked egg, chopped
1/4 teaspoon Worcestershire sauce

- Combine all ingredients in a small bowl. Cover and chill until serving time. Spoon over wedges of iceberg lettuce. Makes about 1 cup

White Chocolate Pie

Serves 6 to 8

A scrumptious dessert that is so simple to make, especially with a store-bought crust. Look for chunks of white chocolate that can be bought in bulk and cost less than packaged.

1 ready made (6 oz.) chocolate crumb crust
1 envelope plain gelatin
1/4 cup cold water
8 ounces white chocolate
1 cup half-and-half
1 teaspoon vanilla extract
small chocolate bar for curls

- Have a chocolate crumb crust ready.
- Stir gelatin into cold water; set aside.
- Chop white chocolate quite small.
- In a saucepan, heat half-and-half until hot but not boiling.
- Add chopped chocolate and stir to dissolve.
- Stir softened gelatin into hot mixture; add vanilla; stir well.
- Cool mixture. Pour into the chocolate crust.
- Chill pie several hours or overnight, until firm.
- Use a vegetable peeler to shave a few long curls from a dark semi-sweet or milk chocolate bar, dropping curls onto top of pie.

> **Chicken Curry on Rice with**
> **Assorted Condiments**
> **Cucumber Raita**
> **Apple or Peach Chutney**
> **Angel Biscuits**
> **Forgotten Cookies**
> **Raspberry or Lime Sherbet**

Chicken Curry on Rice

Serves 4

A spicy, aromatic fragrance fills the air to set the stage for dining on Indian cuisine. You need no special tools or techniques to serve a savory curry with an array of palate teasing condiments .

To prepare the chicken:

> **2 split chicken breasts (1 pound)**
> **3 cups water**
> **A few slices each of onion, carrot, celery**
> **1/2 teaspoon salt**

- Combine and cook over moderate heat until chicken is fork-tender. Cool chicken in broth.

To prepare the curry sauce:

> **3 cups chicken broth from cooking chicken**
> **2 tablespoons butter or margarine**
> **1 cup finely chopped onion**
> **1 small apple, peeled, chopped**
> **1 to 2 tablespoons curry powder**
> **1/4 cup flour**
> **1/3 cup coconut milk (see recipe)**

- Strain cooked chicken, saving broth. Remove skin and bones from chicken; discard. Cut chicken into chunks and reserve.
- Measure broth. If you do not have 3 cups for sauce, dissolve a chicken bouillion cube in enough hot water to add to broth
- Heat a 2-quart pan and melt butter or margarine.
- Add onion and apple; cook over low heat until soft.
- Sprinkle curry powder over onions and stir a few minutes.
- The strength of curry powder varies from mild to hot; add more or less to taste.
- Sprinkle with flour; stir and cook a minute or two.
- Slowly stir in the cooled broth, whisking to keep smooth.
- Cook, whisking occasionally, over low heat, until sauce is thickened and bubbly.
- Whisk in the coconut milk, then add the cut-up chicken.
- This can be done to here the day before. Cover and chill.

To make Coconut Milk:

1 cup boiling water
1/2 cup dried coconut

- Line a small bowl with a double layer of cheesecloth.
- Place coconut on cloth; pour boiling water over.
- Let stand 1 hour or more.
- Lift up edges of cloth and gently squeeze out "milk".
- Empty the dry coconut onto a baking sheet; spread out.
- Bake in a 350° oven until lightly browned. Use as a condiment.
- Serve curry with hot rice and an assortment of condiments guests may choose to sprinkle on top.

Assorted Condiments

Condiments are little palate pleasers that create an extra dimension to a curry dish and are an intregal part of an Indian meal. Offer them in small dishes, choose at least 3 from the list.

Dried coconut	**Sliced banana**
Chopped green onions	**Raisins**
Chutney (see recipe)	**Chopped peanuts**

Cucumber Raita

A cool cucumber sauce that is traditionally served with curries to refresh the palate. Cilantro is also called fresh coriander; it looks like a broad-leafed parsley, but has a more pungent flavor.

1 small cucumber, peeled
1 cup plain low fat yogurt
2 teaspoons vegetable oil (optional)
2 tablespoons chopped fresh mint or cilantro
1/2 teaspoon salt

- Use the coarse side of a grater to shred cucumber.
- Squeeze excess liquid from cucumber.
- Stir together the yogurt, oil, mint or cilantro and salt.
- Mix sauce with cucumber; stir well. Keep chilled.

Apple or Peach Chutney

When I lived in Hawaii, I made mango chutney, scenting the house with aromas from this spicy, chunky condiment. Now I use apples or peaches, unless mangoes are a bargain.

2 pounds apples or peaches, peeled, cored
1 1/2 cups sugar
3/4 cup cider vinegar
1 whole lemon, very thinly sliced
1 inch fresh ginger root, peeled, minced
1 cup onions, chopped small
2 cloves garlic, chopped very fine
1/2 cup raisins or currants
1 teaspoon mustard seeds
1 teaspoon whole cloves
1 teaspoon salt
1/2 teaspoon crushed red pepper flakes
1/2 cup almonds or walnuts, toasted, chopped

- Prepare the apples or peaches, cutting into inch-size chunks, and set aside.
- Cut lemon slices into quarters; remove seeds.
- Combine in a large heavy pan all ingredients except fruit and almonds or walnuts.
- Bring sauce to a boil; add the cut up apples or peaches.
- Reduce heat, partially covering the pan, and cook about 30 to 40 minutes, stirring occasionally and.checking from time to time to see if apples are tender. Fruit should be soft but not mushy.
- Stir in the toasted almonds or walnuts; remove from heat.
- Ladle into pint jars, cover tightly, and refrigerate.
- Chutney develops flavor as it ripens, so is best made several days ahead. This keeps for two weeks in the refrigerator. *This makes about 6 cups.*

Angel Biscuits

Makes 24 biscuits

These thin little biscuits are feather-light, part biscuit and part roll, a delectable addition to any meal.

2 teaspoons quick acting yeast
1/4 cup warm water
1 tablespoon sugar
2 cups unbleached white flour
2 teaspoons baking powder
1 teaspoon salt
3 tablespoons cold butter or margarine
1/2 cup warm milk

- Combine yeast, warm water and sugar. Let stand for 5 minutes
- In a large bowl, measure flour, baking powder, and salt.
- Cut the butter or margarine into the flour mixture with a pastry blender until mixture resembles coarse crumbs.
- Add milk to yeast mixture; stir into flour mixture; stir into a ball.
- Turn dough out on a floured board; sprinkle with a little flour and knead gently a few times.
- Dough can be done to here. Cover tightly and keep in refrigerator overnight. Bring to room temperature to roll out.
- Spray a large baking sheet with nonstick cooking spray.
- Use a floured rolling pin to roll dough out to1/3 inch thick.
- Use a 2-inch round cookie cutter or top of a glass to cut 24 rounds, placing on baking sheet.
- Cover lightly with a towel and let rise 1 hour.
- Heat oven to 425°. Bake10 minutes to golden brown on top.
- Put biscuits into a napkin-lined basket and serve at once.

Forgotten Cookies

Makes 24 cookies

These are a make-the-night-before treat.They are called "forgotten" because you put them in a low oven, turn off the heat, and leave them overnight.

2 egg whites
1/8 teaspoon cream of tartar
2/3 cup sugar
2/3 cup chocolate chips (4 ounces)
1 teaspoon vanilla extract

- Cut brown paper to fit a large baking sheet. Parchment paper may also be used.
- Heat oven to 350°.
- Beat egg whites on medium speed of an electric mixer until frothy.
- Add cream of tartar; continue to beat until soft peaks form.
- Begin to add sugar, a little at a time, shaking it gently on top of egg whites. Continue beating until sugar is used up.
- Beat 2 minutes more to dissolve the sugar. Remove beaters.
- Stir in the chocolate chips and the vanilla.
- Drop mixture by teaspoonful onto prepared baking sheet.
- Put cookies in oven and turn heat off immediately. Do not open oven door; no peeking!
- Leave cookies in oven 12 hours or overnight.
- Lift cookies off paper with a spatula. Store in an airtight tin. These will keep for several days.

London Pub Cabbage Pie
Braised Carrots and Onions
Waldorf Salad with Almonds
Irish Soda Bread
Strawberry Rhubarb Crumble

London Pub Cabbage Pie

Serves 6

English folk thrive on robust country dishes like this; my guests enjoy it, too. Using packaged pie crust saves time, or you can make your own crust.

8 cups cabbage, shredded (1 medium head)
3 tablespoons butter or margarine
1 teaspoon salt
1/8 teaspoon black pepper
2/3 cup cheddar cheese, shredded
2 refrigerated pie crusts (a 15-oz. package)
1 tablespoon milk, for brushing crust

- Melt the butter or margarine in a large skillet over medium low heat, add the cabbage and cook for 15 to 20 minutes until cabbage is softened, stirring occasionally.
- Season cabbage with salt and pepper; stir in the cheese.
- Heat oven to 400°. Have a 9-inch pie pan ready.
- Unfold bottom crust from package into pie pan.
- Put cabbage into crust, arranging top crust to cover cabbage. Pinch crusts together and flute edges between fingers.
- Brush crust with milk and slash several times.
- Bake at 400° about 30 minutes until crust is lightly browned.

Braised Carrots and Onions

Serves 4

Enjoy the downright goodness of simple and inexpensive vegetables braised to maximize their flavors.

4 to 5 medium-size carrots (about 3/4 pound)
2 medium-size onions (about 3/4 pound)
1 tablespoon vegetable oil
1 teaspoon sugar
1/2 teaspoon salt
1/2 cup cooking water or vegetable broth

- Peel carrots, cut lengthwise in half, and cut into 2-inch chunks.
- Peel onions; cut into quarters from root end to stem.
- Bring 2 cups water to a boil; drop in carrots and onions. Boil for 10 minutes and drain well, reserving the water to add later.
- Heat a large, heavy skillet and add the oil and vegetables.
- Cook, shaking pan or turning vegetables, for 5 minutes.
- Sprinkle with sugar and salt, shake pan, cook 2 minutes.
- Add 1/2 cup of the reserved cooking water or broth to pan and reduce heat. Put a cover on the pan but don't close all the way.
- Cook 15 minutes, turning twice. Keep warm until time to serve.
- These can be prepared a day ahead and reheated.

Waldorf Salad with Almonds

Makes 3 cups

This contemporary version of a classic salad is crunchy, colorful and tangy.

2 medium-size red apples, cored, diced
1 tablespoon lemon juice
1/2 cup celery, diced small
1/3 cup light mayonnaise
1/3 cup plain low fat yogurt
1 teaspoon sugar
Pinch of salt or celery salt
2 tablespoons sliced almonds, toasted
Fresh mint leaves for garnish, optional

- Wash the apples but do not peel. Dice into a bowl and sprinkle with lemon juice to prevent their turning dark. Add celery.

- Mix mayonnaise, yogurt, sugar and pinch of salt.

- Toss dressing with apples and celery.

- Cover and keep chilled.

- Arrange a few lettuce leaves on each salad plate: spoon salad onto lettuce.

- Sprinkle sliced toasted almonds over the top of salad.

- Garnish salads with a sprig of fresh mint, if desired.

Helpful Hint

Almonds can be toasted in a microwave by spreading out on a shallow dish and cooking for 1 to 2 minutes. The power of microwave ovens varies; adjust times for your oven.

Irish Soda Bread

Makes 16 slices

Sweetened with raisins, and nourishing with whole wheat flour, this is an easy and tasty bread. It also makes marvelous toast.

2 cups whole wheat flour
1 cup unbleached white flour plus flour for kneading
2 teaspoons baking powder
1 teaspoon baking soda
1 teaspoon salt
2 tablespoons vegetable oil
1 cup buttermilk or light sour cream
1/2 cup currants or seedless raisins

- Heat oven to 375°. Lightly oil a 9-inch pie pan.
- Measure flour, baking powder, soda and salt into a bowl and mix together.
- Stir in the oil and buttermilk or sour cream. Add currants or raisins.
- Lightly flour a work surface and turn dough out.
- Knead just 10 times, adding a little flour as needed. Dough should stay soft; scrape off surface as needed to keep it together.
- Place dough in a pie pan. Pat the top to flatten loaf a little. Slash a cross on top of loaf with the tip of a knife.
- Bake at 375° for 1 hour.
- Remove from pan to cool on a rack.
- For a softer crust, wrap warm loaf in a kitchen towel as soon as you take it from the oven. This loaf can be made the day before. Keep tightly wrapped.

Strawberry Rhubarb Crumble

Serves 6

Rhubarb spells spring to me and I can't resist the first pink stalks that appear in the market. This is adapted from the book "Loving Food" by Sara Jane Kasperzak.

1 pint strawberries, hulled, cut in half
2 cups fresh rhubarb, cut into 1/2 inch pieces
3 tablespoons fresh orange juice
Grated rind of 1 orange
3/4 cup sugar
1/4 cup unbleached white flour

- Butter a deep 2-quart round casserole dish.
- Heat oven to 375°.
- In a bowl, mix strawberries and rhubarb; stir in juice and rind.
- In another bowl, stir together the sugar and flour, pour over fruit and mix gently until fruit is evenly covered. Pour into casserole.

Topping:

1 cup unbleached white flour
1 cup sugar
1/3 cup cold butter or margarine
1 cup milk
Nutmeg to taste

- Stir flour and sugar together; cut in butter with a pastry blender or two knives until mixture is crumbly. Stir in milk.
- Spoon over the fruit and sprinkle with nutmeg.
- Bake 45 minutes. Serve at room temperature.

Super Spicy Baked Chicken
Zucchini Rice Pilaf
Asian Cabbage Salad
Refrigerator Rolls
Pineapple Apricot Upside-down Cake

Super Spicy Baked Chicken

Serves 4

This sauce has a zing and the kitchen smells wonderful as it bakes slowly for 2 hours. The chicken is good served cold, too.

1/4 cup soy sauce
1/2 cup water
2 tablespoons minced ginger root
2 cloves garlic, smashed, chopped
1 tablespoon vegetable oil
2 tablespoons brown sugar
1 teaspoon cayenne pepper
8 chicken thighs or 1 cut-up chicken

- Mix all ingredients for the marinade in a glass or enamel pan and add chicken pieces, turning to coat. Cover. Let stand in refrigerator 5 or more hours, turning chicken from time to time.

- Heat oven to 300°.

- Lightly oil a baking pan; put in chicken. Bake for 2 hours, basting chicken frequently with marinade.

- If you prefer outdoor cooking on a grill, prebake the chicken 30 minutes only. Marinating can be done the day before.

Zucchini Rice Pilaf

Serves 4 to 6

A sprightly rice dish with little green chunks, this pilaf can also be made with broccoli.

4 teaspoons olive oil or butter
1 cup onion, chopped small
1 cup brown or white rice
1 teaspoon salt
2 1/4 cups water or vegetable broth
1 small zucchini (6 ounces), diced small
1 clove garlic, finely chopped
1/4 teaspoon dried thyme
1/4 teaspoon black pepper
1 tablespoon Parmesan cheese

- Heat a 2-quart pan, add half the oil or butter. Add onion and cook 5 minutes, stirring occasionally.

- Stir in rice and salt; cook 1 minute more.

- Add water or broth, cover pan, and simmer until rice is tender and liquid absorbed. This takes about 20 minutes for white rice, 40 minutes for brown.

- In a skillet, heat remaining oil or butter; add garlic, cook 1 minute and add zucchini. Stir-fry a few minutes, add thyme and pepper. Stir into the cooked rice. Transfer to serving dish and sprinkle with the Parmesan cheese.This can be done ahead to here and put into an ovenproof dish. Cover and chill. Bring casserole to room temperature before reheating to serve hot.

- If making pilaf with broccoli instead of zucchini, blanch 4 to 6 ounces of sliced broccoli florets in boiling water for 1 minute before adding to skillet.

Asian Cabbage Salad

Serves 6

Exotic flavors are developed from seasonings in this make-ahead salad. The cabbage is cooked, but still crunchy.

1 tablespoon vegetable oil
1 medium-size onion, thinly sliced
1/2 teaspoon salt
8 cups shredded cabbage (about 1 pound)
1 sweet red or green pepper, cut in thin strips
1 medium-size carrot, shredded coarsely
1 tablespoon ginger root, minced
1 teaspoon turmeric
1 tablespoon vinegar
1 tablespoon soy sauce
2 tablespoons water
1 tablespoon peanut butter
1 teaspoon sugar
1/4 teaspoon crushed red pepper flakes, to taste

- Prepare vegetables. Discard tough outer leaves of cabbage.

- Heat a large skillet or wok and add the oil. Swirl to coat pan, add onion, sprinkle with salt and cook a few minutes.

- Stir in cabbage, red or green pepper and the ginger root.

- Cook 10 minutes, stirring occasionally, until cabbage begins to soften but still is crunchy.

- Sprinkle turmeric on cabbage; toss to mix, cook 2 minutes.

- Stir vinegar, soy sauce, water, peanut butter and sugar together. Add this mixture to pan. Stir in red pepper flakes. Cook 2 minutes.

- Stir in shredded carrot, stir and toss to mix well.

- Put into serving bowl, cover with plastic wrap and chill several hours or overnight. Flavors blend as this perky salad stands. Omit the red pepper flakes if you prefer a milder flavor.

Refrigerator Rolls

Makes 20 rolls

This easy dough can be made several days ahead and will make one large or two smaller batches of crusty hot rolls.

2 teaspoons active dry yeast
1 cup warm water, divided
2 tablespoons sugar
2 tablespoons vegetable oil
2 cups whole wheat flour
1 1/2 to 2 cups unbleached white flour
2 tablespoons sesame or flax seeds, optional

- Combine yeast, sugar and 1/4 cup of the warm water and let stand 5 minutes until foamy.
- Add oil and remaining water and begin to stir in flour.
- Add flour until dough forms a ball, using hands to work flour in.
- Knead lightly on a floured surface for a few minutes.
- Oil dough lightly and transfer to a plastic bag.
- Refrigerate overnight or for 2 to 3 days.
- Two hours before baking, remove dough from refrigerator. Divide in half; refrigerate half. Half the dough makes 10 balls.
- Take a piece of dough and form into a ball between palms of your hands. If dough is sticky, oil your hands. Place balls on a lightly oiled baking sheet.
- If using seeds, put 2 tablespoons of sesame or flax seeds on a saucer; dip balls in seeds, pressing seeds into top of roll.
- Cover; let balls rise until double in size, 60 to 90 minutes.
- Heat oven to 375°. Bake 15 to 20 minutes.

Pineapple Apricot Upside-down Cake
9 pieces

This is an old dessert that brings back memories of childhood, but it takes on new charm and bright color by adding apricots .

9 dried apricot halves
1 can (20 oz.) sliced pineapple, drained
1/2 cup butter or margarine, divided (1 stick)
3/4 cup brown sugar
1 cup white sugar
2 eggs, lightly beaten
2/3 cup milk
2 cups unbleached white flour
3 teaspoons baking powder
1 teaspoon vanilla extract

- Heat oven to 350°.
- Pour 1/2 cup boiling water over apricots; let stand to soften.
- In a 9 x 9-inch pan, melt 2 tablespoons butter or margarine. Sprinkle pan bottom evenly with the brown sugar.
- Drain apricots and arrange evenly on top of brown sugar.
- Place 9 slices of the drained pineapple on top of apricots, overlapping slices slightly.
- Cream remaining butter or margarine with white sugar; add eggs and milk; mix well.
- Stir in flour and baking powder; mix well. Add vanilla.
- Pour cake batter over fruit, spreading evenly.
- Bake for 35 to 40 minutes, until lightly browned on top.
- Remove and cool for 5 minutes. Run a knife around edge of pan to loosen cake. Place a large plate over pan. Invert pan so cake comes out on plate with fruit on top.
- Cut into 9 squares and serve warm.

```
Sweet and Pungent Pork
Marinated Tomato Salad
Scallion Drop Biscuits
Lemon Cheese Pie
```

Sweet and Pungent Pork

Serves 4

When I took Chinese cooking lessons years ago, everyone in the class raved about this recipe. Your guests will rave, too.

3/4 pound pork tenderloin, cut in 1-inch cubes
1 egg, slightly beaten
2 tablespoons unbleached white flour
1/2 teaspoon salt
Vegetable oil for deep frying
2 green peppers
1 medium-size carrot, thinly sliced
1 small can pineapple tidbits
1/2 cup chicken broth
1 can (5 oz.) chow mein noodles for serving

- Cut green peppers into 1-inch diamond shapes.
- Drop peppers and sliced carrots into 1 quart of boiling water and boil 3 minutes. Drain and set aside.
- Mix egg, flour and salt for a batter. Coat pork cubes with batter.
- Heat oil in a saucepan and deep fry pork for about 5 minutes on each side. Set pork on paper towels after frying. Drain oil into a container to save for other frying.
- Leave 1 tablespoon of oil in the pan.
- Add to pan the peppers, carrots, pineapple, pork and broth. Cover. Bring to a boil; lower heat, cook 10 minutes. Pour sweet and sour sauce over pork.

Sweet and Sour Sauce:

2 tablespoons cornstarch
1/2 cup sugar
1/2 cup vinegar
3 tablespoons soy sauce
2/3 cup chicken or vegetable broth

- Mix cornstarch and sugar in a saucepan, then add vinegar, soy sauce and broth. Bring to a boil, stirring to prevent lumps.
- Pour sauce over pork and stir as it cooks to a glaze.
- Serve over chow mein noodles.

Marinated Tomato Salad
Serves 4

When tomatoes are in season there's mint in the garden, too.

2 large red or gold tomatoes, sliced (1 pound)
4 sprigs of fresh mint leaves, chopped
2 tablespoons apple cider vinegar
1 teaspoon honey
1/2 teaspoon salt
1/4 teaspoon dry mustard
1/4 cup vegetable oil

- Mix vinegar, honey, salt and mustard and stir to dissolve.
- Stir in oil and chopped mint. If fresh mint is not available, use fresh basil leaves, cilantro or parsley.
- Arrange slices of tomatoes on a serving plate, alternating colors if you use both red and gold. Cover with just enough dressing to moisten. Top with another layer of tomatoes; sprinkle with dressing.
- Cover and let stand 1 hour at room temperature.
- Just before serving, tuck leaf lettuce under slices for a green ruffled accent to the colorful tomatoes.

Scallion Drop Biscuits

16 to 18 biscuits

Scallions are the very thinnest of young green onions and a nice addition to this crusty little hot bread.

2 cups unbleached white flour
2 teaspoons baking powder
1/2 teaspoon salt
1/2 cup chopped green scallions
1 teaspoon dried dill weed
1/4 cup vegetable oil
3/4 cup milk

- Heat oven to 400°. Lightly oil a baking sheet.

- Measure dry ingredients into a mixing bowl; stir well.

- Stir in scallions and dried dill.

- Add oil and milk, stirring to combine wet and dry ingredients.

- Use a large spoon to drop spoonfuls onto baking sheet.

- Bake in the hot oven 15 to 20 minutes, until lightly browned. Transfer to a napkin-lined basket and serve warm.

Lemon Cheese Pie

6 servings

This rich and creamy dessert offers tantalizing flavors and is so easy to make. It's marvelous in a chocolate crumb crust, too. Use an electric mixer or a food processor to whip up the filling.

Crumb Crust:

16 square graham crackers (about 5 ounces)
3 tablespoons melted butter or margarine
1 tablespoon sugar

- Crush graham crackers or whiz in blender for crumbs.
- Mix butter or margarine and sugar with crumbs.
- Press firmly into 9-inch pie pan. Set aside; prepare filling.

Filling:

8 ounces cream cheese, at room temperature
3 tablespoons fresh lemon juice
1 large egg
1/3 cup sugar
1 teaspoon grated lemon rind

- Heat oven to 350°.
- Beat cream cheese and lemon juice until smooth.
- Beat in the egg and sugar. Add lemon rind; beat until smooth.
- Spoon into the crust. (Use ready-made crumb crust, if desired.)
- Bake pie 15 minutes, remove from oven, and cool 15 minutes.

Topping:

1 cup light sour cream
1 tablespoon sugar
1 teaspoon grated lemon rind

- Mix sour cream, sugar and lemon rind. Pour over prebaked pie.
- Bake 10 minutes, turn off heat and leave pie in oven 5 minutes.
- Remove and cool. Chill 8 hours or overnight.

Chiles Relleno American Style
Baked Stuffed Tomatoes
Brazilian Black Bean Salad
Brown Rice Breadsticks
Cherry Cake with Streusel Topping

Chiles Relleno American Style

Serves 6

Traditional relleno calls for stuffing poblano peppers, dipping them in a batter and deep frying. This way is much easier, and delicious.

2 cans (4 oz. each) whole green chile peppers
6 ounces Monterey Jack cheese, shredded
6 ounces cheddar cheese, shredded
2 eggs, lightly beaten
1 cup evaporated milk
2 tablespoons flour
1/2 teaspoon salt

- Heat oven to 350°. Lightly oil an 8 x 8-inch pan.

- Remove seeds from peppers. Arrange in a layer in the pan.

- Cover with a layer of the cheeses, mixed together.

- Lightly beat the eggs; add milk, flour and salt. Beat well.

- Pour egg mixture gently over peppers and cheeses.

- Bake 45 minutes until set. Cool 5 minutes.

- Cut into squares to serve.

Baked Stuffed Tomatoes

Serves 4

Make the most of fresh garden tomatoes when in season.

4 medium-size tomatoes
1/2 cup onion, chopped
2 teaspoons butter or margarine
1 teaspoon brown sugar
1/2 teaspoon salt
1/2 cup dry soft bread cubes

- Heat oven to 350°. Lightly oil a small baking dish.
- Slice the top off each tomato and gently scoop out the pulp.
- Discard seeds, if desired. Chop the tomato pulp; set aside.
- Heat a small pan and saute the onion in the melted butter until onion is soft. Sprinkle with salt and brown sugar; stir in the tomato pulp and bread cubes.
- Spoon filling into tomato shells. Place in baking dish.
- Bake tomatoes for 30 minutes; serve warm.

Brazilian Black Bean Salad

Serves 4

Colors and flavors sing out in this savory salad to make ahead.

1 can (15 oz.) black beans, drained
1/2 sweet red or green pepper, diced
1/2 cup celery, diced small
1 green onion, thinly sliced
1 tablespoon olive oil
2 teaspoons apple cider vinegar
1/2 teaspoon salt
1/2 teaspoon dried basil
1/4 teaspoon black pepper

- In a glass salad bowl, mix vinegar and seasonings. Add oil.
- Stir in the drained black beans, peppers, celery and onion.
- Cover, chill 30 minutes. Arrange on lettuce leaves.

Brown Rice Breadsticks

Makes 14 breadsticks

A little leftover rice adds fiber to these crunchy breadsticks.

2 teaspoons active dry yeast
2 teaspoons sugar
3/4 cup warm water
1 tablespoon oil
1/2 teaspoon salt
1/2 cup cooked brown rice
1 cup unbleached white flour
2 cups whole wheat flour
1 tablespoon caraway or flax seeds

- Put yeast, sugar and 1/4 cup warm water in a bowl and let stand 5 to 10 minutes until foamy.
- Add remaining water, oil, salt and cooked rice. Stir well.
- Stir in the flour and seeds, adding enough flour to form a soft ball that holds together.
- Turn out on floured surface and knead 5 minutes, working in more flour if needed, until dough is smooth and elastic.
- Put dough into an oiled bowl, turning to coat evenly. Cover bowl and let rise in a warm place until double, 1 hour or more.
- Lightly oil a large baking sheet. Divide dough into 14 balls.
- Roll and stretch each ball into a 10-inch rope; place on pan.
- Let rise 15 to 20 minutes. Heat oven to 375°.
- Bake 15 to 20 minutes, until lightly browned. Using tongs, turn breadsticks over once after 10 minutes.
- Remove from pan.
- These can be baked ahead and reheated in a warm oven just before serving.

Cherry Cake with Streusel Topping

Serves 12

This big crunchy-topped cake is adapted from a recipe by the Cherry Marketing Institute. It's good with blueberry pie filling, too.

Topping:

1/2 cup firmly packed brown sugar
1/3 cup unbleached white flour
1/3 cup old-fashioned or quick-cooking oats
1 teaspoon cinnamon
1/4 teaspoon nutmeg
1/4 cup butter or margarine, softened

Batter:

1 1/2 cups unbleached white flour
1/2 cup sugar
2 teaspoons baking powder
1/2 teaspoon salt
3 tablespoons vegetable oil
2 eggs, lightly beaten
3/4 cup milk
1 can (21 oz.) cherry pie filling

- For the topping, mix dry ingredients and cut in butter or margarine until mixture is crumbly. Set aside.
- Heat oven to 350°. Lightly oil a 11 x 8 x 2-inch baking pan.
- For the batter, combine flour, sugar, baking powder and salt in a large mixing bowl.
- Stir in oil, eggs and milk; mix just until dry ingredients are combined. Batter may be lumpy, do not overmix.
- Spread half the batter in the baking pan. Spoon cherry filling over batter evenly. Spoon on remaining batter.
- Sprinkle the streusel topping mixture over cake batter.
- Bake 30 to 35 minutes, until golden brown on top.
- Cut into squares to serve warm or cold.
- This is great with a scoop of frozen vanilla yogurt or ice cream.

Individual Salmon Loaves with Dill Sauce
Oven Crisp Potato Cubes
Green Beans with Almonds
Carrot Raisin Salad
Peach Cream Pie

Individual Salmon Loaves with Dill Sauce

Serves 4

A piquant sauce brings new interest to the old fashioned goodness of a traditional dish.

1 can (15 oz.) salmon
2 cups cracker crumbs (about 18 saltines)
1/4 cup finely minced onion
2 eggs
1/4 cup milk
2 tablespoons minced parsley
1 tablespoon lemon juice
1/4 teaspoon salt
Pinch of black pepper
4 lemon wedges, for garnish

- Heat oven to 375°. Lightly oil a baking pan.
- Drain salmon, flake and mix with crumbs and onions.
- Beat eggs lightly; add milk, parsley, lemon juice, salt and pepper.
- Combine with salmon and crumb mixture.
- Shape into four oval loaves about 4 inches long, 2 inches wide.
- Bake 30 minutes, until lightly browned on top.
- Lift onto plates; top with the dill sauce.
- Garnish each plate with a sprig of parsley and a lemon wedge.

Dill Sauce

2 tablespoons butter or margarine
2 tablespoons flour
1 cup milk
1 tablespoon lemon juice
1/2 teaspoon salt
1/2 teaspoon dried dill weed

• Melt butter in a saucepan, stir in flour; whisk smooth.

• Whisk in milk; simmer until sauce thickens and bubbles.

• Stir in lemon juice, salt and dill weed. If made ahead, cover, and chill. Reheat over a pan of hot water just before serving.

Oven-Crisp Potato Cubes
Serves 4

Crisp brown cubes with an intriguing flavor.

3 medium-large potatoes (about 1 pound)
2 green onions, sliced 1/4-inch thick
1 tablespoon soy sauce
2 tablespoons vegetable oil
2 tablespoons minced fresh parsley

• Cook potatoes until barely tender; cool, and remove skins.

• Cut potatoes into 1-inch cubes. Keep covered.

• Mix onions, soy sauce and oil in a large bowl. Add the potatoes and stir well to coat. Potatoes can be prepared ahead to here.

• Heat oven to 375°.

• Spray a large baking sheet with nonstick cooking spray and arrange potatoes and onions in a single layer.

• Bake 25 to 30 minutes, turning once with a large spatula.

• Transfer to serving bowl; top with minced parsley.

Green Beans with Almonds

Serves 4

Don't overcook green beans; let them be tender but crisp. Buy raw almonds in bulk, and use in their brown skins.

1 (10-oz.) package French-cut green beans
1/2 teaspoon salt
1 tablespoon butter or margarine
2 tablespoons almonds, thinly sliced

- In a large pan, bring 2 quarts water to a boil; add salt.
- Drop beans into pan and boil just until beans are tender.
- Drain beans at once and keep warm.
- Heat a small skillet, melt butter, add almonds and stir over moderately high heat until just beginning to brown.
- Toss beans with buttered almonds. Serve at once.

Carrot Raisin Salad

Serves 4

As a child, I ate carrots because they were reputed to produce curly hair. As an adult, I love carrots both cooked and raw.

2 cups shredded raw carrots
1/2 cup seedless raisins
1/4 cup mayonnaise
3 tablespoons milk
2 teaspoons lemon juice
1/4 teaspoon salt

- Toss carrots and raisins together.
- Stir together the remaining ingredients.
- Pour over carrots and raisins; mix well.
- Cover and chill.
- This can be prepared hours or a day ahead.

Peach Cream Pie

Serves 6

Celebrate peach season with a yummy dessert. A beginning cook can buy a crust and make this with great success.

One unbaked 9-inch pastry shell
3 large fresh peaches
3/4 cup sugar, divided
2 tablespoons flour
1 cup half-and-half or heavy cream

- Heat oven to 400°.
- Drop peaches into boiling water for 1 minute, remove and slip off skins. Cut peaches in half.
- Place peach halves cut side up in pie shell.
- Sprinkle peaches with 1/4 cup of the sugar.
- Mix 1/2 cup sugar with the flour; stir in the cream.
- Pour the flour and cream mixture over the peaches.
- Bake pie 50 minutes. Transfer to rack to cool.

Basic Pastry Shell:

1 1/4 cups unbleached white flour
1/4 teaspoon salt
1/3 cup vegetable oil
1 tablespoon cold milk, if needed

- Mix flour and salt; stir in oil with a fork. If mixture is dry, sprinkle on milk and stir until dough holds together.
- Turn out on a lightly floured surface and knead just enough to form a compact ball. Don't overknead.
- Wrap in waxed paper and chill 30 minutes.
- Roll between two pieces of waxed paper into a12-inch circle.
- Fit dough into a 9-inch pie pan; fold edges of dough under and pinch between thumb and fingers to flute edge.
- Unbaked shell can be made days or weeks ahead; wrap and freeze until needed. Recipe can be doubled for a two-crust pie.

Jamaican Lentils and Peppers
Beets in Orange Sauce
Cucumber Dill Salad
Baked Bananas
Oatmeal Chocolate Chip Cookies

Jamaican Lentils and Peppers

Serves 4

Ginger and other exotic spices combine to make a memorable main dish from a humble dried legume.

1 cup dried lentils
4 cups water
1 tablespoon olive oil
1 large onion, chopped (about 2 cups)
1 medium-size carrot, thinly sliced
1 teaspoon salt
2 green peppers, thinly sliced
2 cloves garlic, minced
1 tablespoon minced raw ginger root
1 teaspoon turmeric
1 teaspoon dried oregano
1/2 teaspoon ground coriander
1/4 teaspoon crushed red pepper flakes

- Spread lentils on a plate and pick over to remove any stones.
- Rinse lentils well, combine with water in a 2-quart saucepan. Cover, bring to a boil, reduce heat and cook about 30 minutes until lentils are tender. Keep warm, do not drain.
- Heat a wok or large skillet, add oil, onions, carrots, and salt.
- Cook onions 5 minutes, add peppers, garlic, ginger root.
- Reduce heat to low, cook 20 minutes, stir occasionally.
- Sprinkle spices over vegetables, stir, cook 5 minutes.
- Add cooked lentils to skillet, stir well and simmer 10 minutes.
- This can be prepared hours ahead or the day before; flavors mellow on standing.

Beets in Orange Sauce

Serves 4

Fresh or canned beets take on style with a flavorful sauce.

1 can (16 oz.) sliced beets or 1 pound fresh beets
1/2 cup liquid drained from beets
2 teaspoons cornstarch
2 tablespoons orange juice
1 teaspoon minced orange rind
1 teaspoon honey

- If using fresh beets, choose small ones, wash well, and cook whole until tender. Cool, peel and slice. Save 1/2 cup liquid.
- If using canned beets, drain, reserve 1/2 cup liquid.
- Combine in a saucepan the cornstarch and liquid from beets.
- Cook and stir until thickened and bubbling.
- Stir in orange juice, rind and honey. Add beets to sauce to heat through.

Cucumber Dill Salad

Serves 4

Cool, crisp and refreshing, this complements a spicy main dish.

1 medium cucumber
1 green onion, thinly sliced
1/2 teaspoon salt
1/4 cup sour cream
1/2 teaspoon dried dill weed

- Wash cucumber, trim ends and score sides with tines of a fork.
- Slice cucumber into a small bowl; sprinkle with salt. Cover and let stand 30 minutes. Pour off liquid, pressing cucumbers.
- Stir onion, sour cream and dill together; add cucumbers.

Baked Bananas

Serves 4

A simple dessert that brings back memories of sun drenched islands where the bananas might be sprinkled with rum.

4 ripe but firm bananas
Juice of 1 lime
1/4 cup dark brown sugar

- Heat oven to 350°. Butter a 6 x 9-inch baking dish.
- Peel bananas and slice in half lengthwise. Arrange halves on the buttered dish.
- Sprinkle banana halves with lime juice and then the sugar.
- Bake 20 minutes. Serve warm or cool on individual plates.

Oatmeal Chocolate Chip Cookies

Makes 15 cookies

Soft and chewy, these are an easy-to-make treat. For a big batch, double the recipe.

3/4 cup unbleached white flour
3/4 cup old fashioned or quick-cooking oatmeal
1/2 teaspoon baking soda
1/2 cup firmly packed brown sugar
1/2 cup semisweet chocolate chips
1/4 cup butter or margarine, room temperature
1 egg white, lightly beaten
1 teaspoon vanilla extract

- Heat oven to 375°. Have a large baking sheet ready.
- Combine flour, oatmeal, baking soda and the brown sugar. Mix well, add butter or margarine. Stir in chocolate chips, egg white and vanilla.
- Use a tablespoon to shape 15 balls, placing them 2 inches apart on ungreased baking sheet.
- Bake 8 to 10 minutes, until they begin to brown on the edges.
- Gently transfer cookies to a serving plate to cool.

Meatballs Carbonade on Noodles
Patty Pan Squash Saute
Freezable Cabbage Slaw
Rhubarb Cream Pie

Meatballs Carbonade

Serves 4

This entree makes a substantial meal for serious diners. The meat balls may be made hours ahead and baked at dinner time.

2 slices bacon
2 beef bouillon cubes in 1 1/2 cups hot water
1 pound ground beef
1 egg, slightly beaten
1/4 cup dry bread crumbs
1/2 teaspoon salt
2 tablespoons minced fresh parsley
2 large onions, thinly sliced
2 tablespoons flour
1 teaspoon vinegar
1 teaspoon brown sugar
1/4 teaspoon dried thyme
Salt and pepper to taste for sauce
12 oz. medium-broad noodles

- Cook bacon until crisp, drain on paper towels, crumble and set aside. Reserve 1 tablespoon of the drippings for the gravy.

- In a large bowl, mix 1/4 cup of broth with the ground beef, adding egg, crumbs, salt, and parsley. Form into small balls. Shaping meatballs is easier if you rub ice cubes on your hands.

- Heat pan with remaining drippings; brown balls on all sides. Lift out with a slotted spoon to a casserole dish as they brown.

- Fry onions in the same skillet until tender, put over meatballs.

- Whisk flour into tablespoon of drippings, add remaining broth.

- Whisk in vinegar, sugar and thyme and cook until sauce is thick. Then pour sauce over meatballs and onions. Cover.

- Bake at 350° for 30 minutes, until sauce bubbles.

- Cook 12 ounces medium broad noodles, drain. Arrange in a ring on platter. Fill with meat balls, sprinkle on bacon.

Pattypan Squash Sauté

Serves 4

If you haven't tried this little scallop-edged pale green summer vegetable, you have a treat in store.

2 medium-size pattypan squash
1 tablespoon butter or margarine
Salt and pepper to taste

- Rinse squash; trim off stems. Lay squash flat and slice about 1/4 inch thick, then cut slices in half crosswise.
- Heat a large skillet; melt butter or margarine and swirl pan to coat bottom.
- Add squash slices and saute quickly until slices begin to brown. Don't overcook; squash should be tender but still crisp.
- Sprinkle with salt and pepper and serve at once.

Freezeable Cabbage Slaw

Serves 8

If you divide this into two containers before freezing, you have salad made ahead for two dinners. It has zero fat.

8 cups cabbage, shredded (about 1 pound)
1 medium-size carrot, shredded
1 green pepper, shredded
1 teaspoon salt
1 cup apple cider vinegar
1 cup sugar
1 teaspoon prepared yellow mustard
1 teaspoon celery seed

- Mix vegetables and salt in a large bowl and let stand 1 hour.
- Combine in a saucepan vinegar, sugar, mustard and celery seed. Bring to a boil, reduce heat and simmer 1 minute. Let mixture stand 30 minutes until lukewarm.
- Pour lukewarm dressing over cabbage; mix well.
- Put salad in one or two plastic freezer bags and freeze. Before serving, remove from freezer and let thaw several hours.

Rhubarb Cream Pie

Serves 6 to 8

One of the first fruits of spring, rhubarb has an interesting tart flavor, sweetened in this old family recipe.

Pastry for double crust 9-inch pie (page 145)
3 to 4 stalks fresh rhubarb (3/4 to 1 pound)
1 1/2 cups sugar
3 tablespoons flour
1/2 teaspoon nutmeg
1 tablespoon melted butter or margarine
2 eggs, lightly beaten
1 tablespoon milk for top crust

- Heat oven to 450°.

- Wash rhubarb stalks, but do not peel. Trim tough ends. Cut rhubarb into half-inch pieces. Drain well.

- Line a 9-inch pie pan with bottom crust and add rhubarb.

- In a mixing bowl, stir together the sugar, flour and nutmeg.

- Whisk in the melted butter and eggs.

- Pour the batter over the rhubarb.

- Place top crust over filling; crimp edges of crusts together.

- Brush top crust with milk; slash in several places.

- Place pie in hot oven and immediately reduce the heat to 350°. Bake pie for 40 to 45 minutes.

Chicken Breasts in Supreme Sauce
Golden Potato Slices
Green Beans Vinaigrette
Fudge Brownie Pie

Chicken Breasts in Supreme Sauce

Serves 4

A rich, creamy sauce with the tang of lemon complements the mild flavor of chicken breasts poached in a vegetable broth.

1 pound boneless, skinless chicken breasts
2 cups water
1 onion, roughly cut up
1 large carrot, cut up
1 rib celery with leaves, cut up
1 teaspoon salt

- Put chicken, water, vegetables and salt in pan, bring to a boil, reduce heat. Simmer until breasts are tender, about 30 minutes.
- Strain broth and save for making the sauce.
- Break chicken into 2-inch pieces, removing any pieces of white cartilage. Keep warm until sauce is made.

Supreme Sauce:

2 tablespoons butter or margarine
1 tablespoon flour
1 cup chicken broth (see above)
1 egg, slightly beaten
Juice of half a lemon
1/2 teaspoon salt, if needed
Pinch of cayenne pepper

- Melt the butter, whisk in flour, cook a minute; add broth.
- Whisk until thickened. Pour a little of the sauce into the egg, mix well and then stir all of the egg mixture back into pan.
- Cook sauce a few minutes, stirring. Add lemon juice and cayenne. Taste, adding salt if needed; add chicken.

Golden Potato Slices

Serves 4

Tender insides, crisp on the outside, these elongated oval slices are attractive on the plate. Parboiling the potatoes will insure tenderness. A garnish of fresh herbs adds excitement.

3 large russet potatoes (1 1/2 pounds)
Nonstick cooking spray
Paprika
2 tablespoons minced fresh rosemary or parsley
Salt and pepper to taste

- Scrub potatoes and drop into boiling water. Cook until almost but not quite tender. Remove and cool. Slip off skins.

- Heat oven to 450°. Spray a large baking sheet with nonstick cooking spray.

- Slice potatoes lengthwise about one-third inch thick. Arrange slices of potatoes on pan in a single layer, overlapping slightly.

- Spray again and sprinkle with paprika.

- Bake for about 20 minutes, until golden brown.

- Sprinkle with minced fresh rosemary or parsley.

- Add a sprinkle of salt and pepper. Serve hot.

- Other fresh herbs can be used; try fresh basil or cilantro.

Green Beans Vinaigrette

Serves 4

Garden fresh, young tender beans are perfect for this salad. Pick them in a friend's garden or choose with care at the produce market. A combination of young green beans and yellow wax beans is attractive, but cook each variety separately.

1 pound young thin green beans, or green and yellow wax beans
1/2 teaspoon salt
3 tablespoons olive oil
2 tablespoons white vinegar
1/8 teaspoon black pepper
8 small cherry tomatoes (optional)

- Trim ends from beans and rinse.
- Heat a large kettle of water to boiling, drop in green beans and cook only 2 to 3 minutes. Taste a bean to check doneness.
- Drain while they are still crisp.
- Cook wax beans 2 to 3 minutes; taste to check doneness.
- Drain and mix with the green beans.
- Toss drained beans with the olive oil; cover and set aside.
- This can be done to here hours in advance.
- Just before serving, sprinkle with the vinegar, toss, and add salt to taste and the black pepper.
- Small cherry tomatoes make a colorful garnish.

Fudge Brownie Pie

Serves 8

A dense, moist chocolatey dessert that can be truly decadent if it is cut into wedges, topped with a scoop of praline or coffee ice cream and served with warm chocolate sauce.

1 cup sugar
1/2 cup unsweetened cocoa powder
3/4 cup unbleached white flour
1/4 teaspoon salt
1 egg, lightly beaten
1 teaspoon vanilla extract
1/4 cup vegetable oil
1/4 cup low-fat vanilla yogurt
1/2 cup toasted walnuts or pecans

- Heat oven to 350°. Lighty butter a 9-inch pie pan.
- Mix sugar, cocoa, flour and salt.
- Beat egg lightly; add the vanilla, oil and yogurt.
- Add dry ingredients to egg mixture.
- Mix until moistened; stir in toasted nuts.
- Spread batter in pan. Bake 25 to 30 minutes. Do not overbake. Top will spring back when lightly touched with a fingertip and pie will begin to pull away from the sides of the pan. Cool.
- To serve, cut into wedges. If made ahead, keep covered until time to serve.This can be made the day before and refrigerated.